797,885 Books

are available to read at

Forgotten Books

www.ForgottenBooks.com

Forgotten Books' App
Available for mobile, tablet & eReader

ISBN 978-1-330-94773-9
PIBN 10125040

This book is a reproduction of an important historical work. Forgotten Books uses state-of-the-art technology to digitally reconstruct the work, preserving the original format whilst repairing imperfections present in the aged copy. In rare cases, an imperfection in the original, such as a blemish or missing page, may be replicated in our edition. We do, however, repair the vast majority of imperfections successfully; any imperfections that remain are intentionally left to preserve the state of such historical works.

Forgotten Books is a registered trademark of FB &c Ltd.
Copyright © 2017 FB &c Ltd.
FB &c Ltd, Dalton House, 60 Windsor Avenue, London, SW19 2RR.
Company number 08720141. Registered in England and Wales.

For support please visit www.forgottenbooks.com

1 MONTH OF FREE READING

at
www.ForgottenBooks.com

By purchasing this book you are eligible for one month membership to ForgottenBooks.com, giving you unlimited access to our entire collection of over 700,000 titles via our web site and mobile apps.

To claim your free month visit:
www.forgottenbooks.com/free125040

* Offer is valid for 45 days from date of purchase. Terms and conditions apply.

English
Français
Deutsche
Italiano
Español
Português

www.forgottenbooks.com

Mythology Photography **Fiction** Fishing Christianity **Art** Cooking Essays **Buddhism** Freemasonry Medicine **Biology** Music **Ancient Egypt** Evolution Carpentry Physics Dance Geology **Mathematics** Fitness Shakespeare **Folklore** Yoga Marketing **Confidence** Immortality Biographies Poetry **Psychology** Witchcraft Electronics Chemistry History **Law** Accounting **Philosophy** Anthropology Alchemy Drama Quantum Mechanics Atheism Sexual Health **Ancient History** **Entrepreneurship** Languages Sport Paleontology Needlework Islam **Metaphysics** Investment Archaeology Parenting Statistics Criminology **Motivational**

AUTHOR'S PREFACE.

Believing that earnest Patrons of Husbandry would be interested in perusing a history of the origin, and the early days, of our Order, I was constrained to prepare this little brochure and send it out on its mission of information, trusting that it would receive kindly consideration at the hands of the Grange fraternity. It makes no claim to literary merit or embellishment, nor does it undertake to give a history of the Order, or of the things accomplished by the Order, during all the years since its organization. It would take a volume of much larger dimensions to chronicle, even briefly, the things accomplished by the Grange in the farmers' interests. But it does claim to give a concise, accurate and unembellished account of the foundation of the Grange and a somewhat detailed history of the first decade or so of its existence.

In the preparation of the manuscript for this little History, I was kindly given access to all the original documents and the hundreds of letters written by the "Founders" of the Order, which are still in the possession of Brother O. H. Kelley of Washington, D. C., and to his "History of the Grange" I am indebted for much of the historical information herein presented. From other sources, particularly from those who were indirectly associated with the organization in its early years, much has been learned which I now pass along to Patrons of Husbandry everywhere, that they may know of the struggles and triumphs, the successes and failures, the hopes and fears of the founders of the Grange. May it not teach us still greater reverence for those who, in those early years, builded even better than they knew, and inspire in us all a loftier appreciation of the noble precepts of our beneficent Order!

J. WALLACE DARROW.

Chatham, N. Y., Nov. 1, 1904.

CHAPTER I.

Origin of the Order of Patrons of Husbandry.

> " *With something of the seer*
> *Must the moral pioneer*
> *From the future borrow.*
> *Clothe the waste with dreams of grain*
> *And on the midnight's sky of rain*
> *Paint the golden morrow.*"

IT is given to but few men to set in motion great humanizing forces, agencies or influences; to be founders, builders, organizers, for humanity's sake. Such men must have the prophet's vision coupled with the prophet's faith. They must be altruists in deed as well as in word. Their station is at the threshold of new Eras; their names mark new Epochs. They may dream dreams and see visions, but they bring things to pass. Such a man was Oliver H. Kelley, the originator and first among the founders of the Order of Patrons of Husbandry.

On October 20, 1865, Isaac Newton, then United States Commissioner of Agriculture, wrote to Mr. Kelley, who was then at his home in Itasca, Minn., to come to Washington "on special business." He responded and, on January 1, 1866, received his commission as special agent of the Agricultural Department "to proceed immediately through the states lately in hostility against the Government" to procure statistical and other information bearing upon the agricultural resources of the South, and to report the same to the Department for publication. On January 13, 1866, Mr. Kelley left Washington on his "long cherished trip," as he styles it, and, while absent on that occasion, conceived the idea of a secret organization of farmers, North and South, to renew and promote a more fraternal feeling.

There was need of it. Six months prior to the date of Commissioner Newton's letter to Mr. Kelley, or on April 9, 1865, Lee had surrendered to Grant at Appomattox. On April 14th President Lincoln was shot. Public feeling was intense. The nation was stirred to its depths. Agriculture was a thing quite forgotten. The devastated farms of the South bore crops of cannon balls instead of cotton bolls.

Of this period, National Master J. J. Woodman said in his annual address in 1885 concerning Mr. Kelley's travels:

Although the garments dyed in blood had passed away, and the country was again undivided and indivisible, yet in his southern travels blackened ruins, abandoned fields and desolate homes met his gaze on every hand. The South, and no small portion of the North, was furrowed with graves, and the whole land was shrouded with mourning, and peopled with crippled, wounded and dying soldiers, while in thousands of desolated homes "grief was completing the carnage of war;" and a deep and intense bitterness engendered by the events of the cruel and unnatural struggle existed between the people of the North and South. With Mr. Kelley's observing habits and active mind, he naturally took in the situation, and came to the conclusion (using his own language) "that politicians would never restore peace in the country, and if it came at all, it must come through fraternity; the people North and South must know each other as members of a great family, and all sectionalism be abolished." He expressed these sentiments in a letter written while in the South, and to his friend, the Rev. John Trimble, an officer in the Treasury Department, on his return to Washington; and then went to his farm in Minnesota. He must have seen in his homeward travels that poverty and the depressed condition of farmers was not confined to the South alone; for on the rich prairies and all along the valleys and hill-sides of the West could be seen farmers living in hovels, before which, as Whittier says, "A tree casts the tremulous shadow of its leaves across the curtainless window, from the broken panes of which flutter the signal rags of poverty;" while their rickety barns were fairly bursting with the products of their labor, and the men who handled and manipulated these poor farmers' grain were living in palaces, surrounded with all that wealth and luxury could afford. In all this he saw a great wrong, and became more deeply impressed with the necessity of an organization among farmers, for the protection of their interests, education and elevation of their class, and for restoring friendly feelings and unity of action between the people of the North and the South.

That a fraternal organization of farmers would promote a better feeling between the two sections so lately engaged in a fratricidal strife, was an idea that bore much fruit in the after years. And that an organization having the bond of secrecy as one of its chief features would insure a better fraternity of feeling and a more cordial unison of purposes than an organization non-secret in its character, was the wise conclusion reached by Mr. Kelley from the experiences growing out of his connection with the Masonic Order.

Any history of the Order of Patrons of Husbandry must, of necessity, be a history of the life of Oliver H. Kelley between the years 1866 and 1873. This fact should be borne in mind as the reader progresses in the perusal of this little book, and it will account for the frequent mention of his name. He was the moving spirit of the enterprise and the only man connected with the very early days of the movement who never lost faith in it. "Give him my kind regards," wrote his coadjutor, John Trimble, to another gentleman, "and tell him that although he is an engine with too much steam on all the time, yet with McDowell as the 'governor' I don't think the boiler will burst."

On April 21, 1866, Mr. Kelley returned to Washington from his southern trip and before going to his home in Minnesota, proceeded to Boston, Mass., to visit his niece, Miss Caroline A. Hall, at which time he explained to her his plans for the new organization, and it was she who then suggested that women be given full and equal right of membership in the Order.

In May, 1867, Mr. Kelley made the acquaintance of W. M. Ireland, Chief Clerk of the Finance Office of the Post Office Department, to whom he explained his "new idea" and, in July, William Saunders, head of the Government Experiment Gardens and Grounds, was taken into the "secret," making, with John Trimble and Miss Hall, the five names earliest associated in the history and work of the Order.

It may be well at this point to give an outline of the plans and purposes of these originators of the Order to see just what they proposed to accomplish. The Order was to embrace in its membership only those persons "directly interested in cultivating the soil." It was to be a secret order with four degrees, representing the four seasons, with appropriate signs and pass words; the lectures in each degree were to appertain to agricultural work and, at the same time, convey a moral lesson. The aim was to advance agriculture by encouraging education and to secure to members the same benefits in certain respects as those guaranteed by Masonry. Both sexes were to be admitted, and there were to be separate ceremonies for the ladies. Politics and religion were not to be subjects of discussion. The plan of work was outlined in this manner: To have a temporary organization known as the "United States Lodge," which would have authority to grant dispensations to lecturers and organizers in the several counties in each state; these county organizations were to elect one delegate each to the state organization, and the state organizations one each to the United States organization. The grand head of the organization was to be auxiliary to the Department of Agriculture. Lecturers were to be sent out to explain the purposes of the organization and to secure members.

From a letter written to Mr. Anson Bartlett of North Madison, Ohio, September 2, 1867, by Mr.

Kelley, we discover what high hopes the writer had for his new organization. "In twelve months," said he, "we should number our brothers by the million." It was in the same letter that Mr. Kelley brought out another fact, i. e., that he had associated with him in his work two brother Masons, Ireland and Trimble, whose counsel he needed, particularly in preparing the ritualistic work.

The selection of a name or title for the Order gave the early founders much perplexity. In this matter, as in many others in the early days of the organization, Anson Bartlett of Ohio proved a wise counsellor. In a letter to Mr. Kelley, dated September 15, 1867, he said: "You have struck a plan which will, when fully inaugurated, be a truly splendid thing and must very soon, if properly perfected in all its details, become a tremendous power in the land. We should organize such an institution as will stand the test of age and experience." In the matter of a name for the organization, he said: "Would it not be better to drop the name 'lodges' and substitute the 'farm,' 'garden' or 'vineyard'?" He suggested as a name for the Order "Independent Farmers." To this Mr. Kelley replied, saying that probably fifty names had been suggested. Among them were "Independent Order of Agriculturists", "Progressive Farmers", "Knights of the Plow", "Knights of the Sickle", "Knights of the Flail", etc. In a later letter to Mr. Bartlett, Mr. Kelley suggested the name, "League of Husbandry", and said: "If any original name in place of 'league' could be substituted, it would be better." In a still later letter he advocated the change of the name of 'lodges' to 'granges.' On November 6th Mr. Bartlett replied: "How about the name? How would 'Patrons of Industry' do? I almost fancy it would be good. I believe it is original at any rate." Mr. Kelley accepted the suggestion, in part, but combined the two titles, "League of Husbandry" and "Patrons of Industry" into the one title under which the Order was formally launched, i. e., "Patrons of Husbandry."

It was evident that to give the work a start outside, an organization should be perfected in Washington. All the meetings thus far held had been decidedly informal, not more than three or four persons being present at one time. The first meeting which was at all formal was held November 15, 1867. William M. Ireland presided and O. H. Kelley acted as secretary. A committee was appointed to draw up a preamble, setting forth the object for which the Order was established, and it was decided to adopt the title "Patrons of Husbandry" as the name of the Order and the branches were to be known as "granges." A short time afterward a motto was decided upon, i. e., "ESTO PERPETUA," meaning "Let it be Perpetual!" A copy of the constitution had been sent to Miss Hall of Boston for her examination. In the constitution the membership fee was made ten dollars for males and five dollars for females. On this point she wrote: "Do not get the price of membership too high. Remember dollars are not over plenty among farmers. They are not found on every bush. Five dollars is enough for men and I should say women for half of that. They cannot obtain but half the wages men receive. It is a shame, but I hope the Society will correct the wrong."

Her letter was influential in having the fee reduced.

On December 4, 1867, a meeting for the election of officers of the National Grange, and for the transaction of other business, was held. The following officers were elected:

Master—William M. Ireland, Washington.
Overseer—Anson Bartlett, North Madison, Ohio.

Lecturer—J. R. Thompson, Washington.
Steward—Wm. Muir, St. Louis, Mo.
Secretary—O. H. Kelley, Washington.
Treasurer—William Saunders, Washington.
Assistant Steward—A. S. Moss, Fredonia, N. Y.

The offices of Chaplain and Gate Keeper were left vacant.

About this time the Rev. A. B. Grosh, of Washington, joined the Order, was chosen Chaplain and became quite active in the work.

It was determined to organize a subordinate Grange in Washington as a school of instruction for drill in ritualistic work. In order to get a somewhat larger working body, several gentlemen and their wives were admitted without fee for the service they would render.

From the original minutes of the secretary, the following interesting record is taken:

It was all important that a subordinate Grange should be made up in which to give our degree work a test and see what was wanting. In compiling the degrees, I had pinned up on the wall, near my table, a large plan of a hall with the position of the officers; also a photographic view of the decorated hall of the Philadelphia Pomological Society. I was thus enabled to take my candidates, in imagination, from one officer to the other. To make up a sub Grange needed individuals. Ireland agreed to act as Master and I as Assistant Steward. Faris, an old room mate at a previous date, agreed to join in as Gate Keeper, both of the National Grange and our sub Grange. At this time Saunders suggested the propriety of inviting Rev. A. B. Grosh to join in with us as we had conversed with him and he had expressed such a desire. In a few days I had enlisted some of our fellow clerks in the Post Office Department and we agreed to meet in a room occupied by a part of the Department of Agriculture.

The gentlemen above referred to were J. Espy Douglass, W. G. Perry, A. F. Moulton, J. H. Cook, B. C. Major and H. Dingman. This Grange was known as Potomac No. 1, its principal object being, as before stated, to instruct the members in the degree work and to enable them to assist in organizing granges in other places. It was decided to have seven degrees. The seventh, or Degree of Demeter, embraced features that were taken from an ancient association once flourishing in the East, and F. M. McDowell was appointed High Priest of Demeter. The degrees were as follows :

SUBORDINATE GRANGE.

1st Degree :   Laborer (male) ; Maid (female).
2d Degree :   Cultivator (male) ; Shepherdess (female).
3d Degree :   Harvester (male) ; Gleaner (female).
4th Degree :   Husbandman (male) ; Matron (female).

STATE GRANGE.

5th Degree : Pomona. (Hope.) Composed of Masters and Past Masters of Subordinate granges who are entitled, ex-officio, to the Fifth Degree.

NATIONAL GRANGE (COUNCIL).

6th Degree : Flora. (Charity.) Composed of Masters and Past Masters of State granges who are entitled, ex-officio, to the Sixth Degree, and they should meet annually. They were to constitute the National Council.

SENATE.

7th Degree : Ceres. (Faith.) Composed of members of the Council who have served one year therein, who, after the expiration of their first year's service in the Council, are entitled, ex-officio, to the Seventh Degree, to be conferred at the next or any subsequent session of the National Grange.

It was the intention of the originators to add other degrees as the Order progressed, similar to the Masonic. For instance, the Eighth Degree was to be known as the "Degree of the Golden Sheaf " ; Seventh Degree members to be eligible who were also Priests of Demeter. But the " Golden Sheaf " degree was never formulated.

Those specially interested in the ritual work will be

glad to learn that most of the lectures in the four subordinate degrees were compiled by Mr. Kelley and Miss Hall, with some assistance from Mr. Bartlett and Mr. Ireland. The degree work for the women's degrees was very largely contributed by Miss Hall. Mr. Kelley and Miss Hall wrote all of the Fifth Degree. The Sixth and Seventh degrees are both commonly accredited to Mr. J. R. Thompson, for which work he received $500 from the National Grange. It was ten years after Fredonia Grange No. 1 was organized, before the ritual was really completed and perfected. At the present writing (1904) the National Grange has its further revision under consideration. It may be stated here that it was the original intention of the authors of the ritual to have all of the degrees worked out of doors, but for obvious reasons this idea did not prevail. The Preamble to the Constitution was written by Mr. Saunders and the Declaration of Purposes by Mr. J. W. A. Wright of California.

The invocation of the Chaplain used in the opening of every Grange meeting was penned by Mr. Kelley, and it was almost the final work on the ritual. Mr. Kelley tells a little story of how he wrote it. In conversation with Dr. Trimble one day, he said to him: "Doctor, you haven't written anything for the ritual and you must write the opening invocation." Mr. Trimble (who, by the way, was a clergyman) replied that he must be excused. But the time was near at hand when the work must be closed up and sent to the printers. On retiring that night Mr. Kelley was puzzled over the matter. He did not sleep. His thoughts were on this last important subject. As he thought, sentences began to formulate themselves, words dropped into their proper places and, arising quickly from his bed, he took pencil and paper and wrote what is now, and ever has been, the opening invocation used by Grange chaplains as they implore Divine direction in the labors of the Grange.

In February of 1868 Mr. Kelley resigned his position in the Post Office Department, which he had held during 1867, and gave his entire time to the work of establishing the Order. He gave much attention to perfecting the ritual. He believed it would add to the interest of the work to establish a regular subordinate Grange in Washington, which was done, and it was given the name of Harvest Grange. It was really the school of instruction before established, and which was called Potomac Grange.

On February 19th, at a meeting of Harvest Grange; the first man ever initiated in due form into the Order received his first degree—a Mr. Boardman of New York. The work was done exclusively from manuscript copies, about thirty brothers and sisters being present, in numbers about equally divided, and all expressed themselves as highly pleased with the working of the degree.

The subject of the extension of the Order by organizing granges outside of Washington now impressed itself upon the active workers at Washington. A meeting of the National Grange was held March 28, 1868 (present, Messrs. Saunders, Trimble, Grosh, Ireland, Thompson, Kelley). It was decided to give the Secretary a "letter of credit" for the purpose of enabling him to organize the Order in the various states. It was, however, of no particular value to him, as he remarked that "pluck and perseverance were more valuable requisites." He was instructed as to the manner of imparting the degree and was allowed discretionary power in all the work, and he was voted a salary of $2,000 per annum and necessary traveling expenses, but the National Grange wished it to be explicitly understood that its officers were "not held personally responsible for the salary or expenses."

The time for missionary work had come; someone must go out into the field and reap the harvest these enthusiastic founders of the Order believed to be ready for gathering, so, on the afternoon of April 3, 1868, Secretary Kelley started for Harrisburg, Pa. He relates an amusing interview with Mr. Saunders. He was seated at his desk, and as he handed him some blank dispensations to sign, Mr. Kelley remarked, in a joking way :

" Here I am, ready to start."

"Start for where ? " Mr. Saunders asked.

" I have bought a ticket for Harrisburg and stop there the first place. I propose to work my way to Minnesota, organizing granges."

" Have you got any money ? "

" I have about two dollars and a half of Grange funds, but intend to pay my way as I go."

In a pleasant way he said : " Well, you are a fool to start on such a trip."

"Can't help that ; fool or no fool, you shall hear from me, and I'll make the Order a success or burst."

The faith of this man was remarkable, for there were discouraging times before him such as he scarcely dreamed of, but perseverance such as his overcomes all obstacles, and he went out to the work in Faith and in Hope.

CHAPTER II.

Extension of the Order.

APRIL 3, 1868, marks the second Epoch in the work of organization. There had been some correspondence with people residing outside of Washington city relative to the establishing of the Grange elsewhere, but not until that date had there been special attention given to this work. It was on the evening of that day that Mr. Kelley left Washington for Harrisburg, Pa., little dreaming, as he says, of the amount of hard work that was to accompany the task he had undertaken or that months would become years before success would follow. He attempted to organize a Grange at Harrisburg but did not succeed. He says, "There was a skeleton in the closet." From Harrisburg he went to Penn Yan, N. Y., and thence to Wayne, N. Y., where he met F. M. McDowell, who encouraged him on his way in a very substantial manner by giving him $50, as well as cheering words. He made an attempt to establish a Grange at Penn Yan and failed. But at Fredonia, N. Y., where he arrived on April 15, he did succeed, and there and then was established the first regularly organized Grange in the United States, or in the world, whose members paid initiation fees. This was the real foundation of the Order. It may be of interest here to give the names of those who were the organizers of that original Grange. They were A. S. Moss, H. Stiles, W. H. Stevens, U. E. Dodge, L. McKinstry,

A. P. Bond, D. Fairbanks, W. McKinstry, Wm. Risley and M. S. Woodford. U. E. Dodge was elected Master.

Twenty-five years after that date, on April 20 and 21, 1893, the Silver Jubilee of Fredonia Grange No. 1 was celebrated. An elaborate program covering the two days was presented, addresses being made by E. P. Harris of Brockton, N. Y., E. B. Hewes, L. McKinstry, O. H. Kelley, Mrs. B. B. Lord, U. E. Dodge, W. C. Gifford, H. H. Goff, J. D. F. Woolston and several others. A letter was read from Miss Caroline A. Hall, who was then residing in Minneapolis, Minn. It is interesting to note two or three facts stated in Mr. Kelly's address on that occasion. He said that in the first year only 10 dispensations were issued ; the second, 36 ; the third, 134. At the end of the fourth year there were in all 1,005, but in 1874 there was marvelous progress made, and they averaged over 2,000 new granges a month. During the twelve years which he held the position of National Secretary, and during which time Miss Hall was his assistant, $400,000 was received, and at the end of that period the committee published a report showing the National Grange had no outstanding obligations.

From Fredonia, Mr. Kelley went to Spencer, Ohio, the home of Anson Bartlett, who had already been interested in the work by correspondence. This visit was an agreeable one to Mr. Kelley, and he instructed Mr. Bartlett in the work of organization and left him to introduce it in that part of the State. From Spencer, Mr. Kelley went to Chicago. There he met Mr. H. D. Emery of the "Prairie Farmer," with whom he had previously corresponded with reference to organizing a Grange there. He says that he met several persons that evening and made them familiar with the ritual, but a grange was not then organized. From there he went to Madison-

Wis., where after four days' work he met with failure. A rather amusing letter written at that time to Mr. McDowell gives very well Mr. Kelley's idea of the people whom he met at that time and one of whom he referred to as his "pompous friend" (the man with whom he had previously corresponded). This gentleman remarked to him that the Order "might be of great advantage in country towns but not in cities like Madison." Madison had 1,800 votes. He left Madison for St. Paul, near which place was his home. Eleven months had passed since leaving his family; he thought a rest would do him good. While there he received a letter from A. Failor of Newton, Iowa, informing him that a Grange had been organized at that place, the first Grange in Iowa and the first application by letter ever received for a dispensation.

The first person ever obligated and instructed in the ritual in Minnesota was Miss Julia Wilkin Kelley, daughter of O. H. Kelley. She it was who officiated as Pomona in the State Grange of Minnesota on the first evening the Fifth Degree was ever conferred.

While we leave Mr. Kelley resting at his home in Minnesota, it may be interesting to note what the so-called National Grange was doing at Washington these days. That it was doing almost nothing is evidenced by the letters which passed between some of the "organizers" and Mr. Kelley. It is to be borne in mind that these were all busy men connected with some of the governmental departments and doubtless had not the time to give much attention to the work. The following paragraph taken from a letter by Dr. Trimble to Mr. Kelley shows his feeling relative to taking an active interest in the Order at that time, although, as all Patrons know, he was in later years Secretary of the National Grange and a most interested and efficient worker in the Order. Nevertheless at this time he often styled himself a critic of the movement and his strong forte seemed to be, as he often said, "to throw a wet blanket" on the discussions. The paragraph is as follows:

"I know nothing, absolutely nothing, about the Order here, and am not able to take any part in the matter. This you are aware of, for I never hesitated to say so to you. So you must not hold me accountable for inaction here. I have nothing whatever to do with the active or actual work of the Order. Please bear this in mind."

Mr. Kelley was unable to interest the Washington gentlemen in pushing the work of securing new members, and this greatly annoyed him. He realized the importance of having strong men as backers and their dilatoriness in replying to his communications and their general lack of interest in the work drew from him the following letter, dated at Itasca, Minn., July 12, 1868:

To the Officers of the National Grange.

Worthy Brothers,—When I left Washington three months ago you all said the Patrons were a success. I felt encouraged; I presumed the interest shown would be kept up by you all. There were in Washington at least some thirty or forty interested persons. As I understand the matter, you have not added a member since I left, but sat down to see what I was doing—watching my progress, and looking to my labors alone to pay all bills and keep the thing running. I hope you will duly consider this, and now that I am in a very unpleasant situation, trust you will be lenient. I do not expect any pecuniary assistance from the Order, but I certainly have a right to expect the National Grange will take some active interest in the work. Can you not delegate some of those familiar with the work, who may go into the country this summer, to organize where they go? Every Grange started helps us all. You see what I am doing. I have accepted the position of associate editor of a small paper here, with a brother Patron, and we are determined to help the work. I have added this extra work for the good of the cause, and have no remuneration for it. You must show some active interest in the work, for wherever I go I speak of The National Grange. You can see that my efforts will avail nothing if upon inquiry they learn there is no interest taken by you. I tell you now, as I told you before, you have a good thing—a big thing—if you will only be active. * * * * Don't delay—action is now necessary. Have faith ; faith will remove mountains. Assist me in this way and we will soon have funds enough. We must come out bold, and by so doing the leading political papers will start out, some for and some against; but no matter—it will advertise the Order. Let what you say be something tangible, that will take with the laboring classes, and we are sure to win. Come down among the people ; don't stay up among the politicians. Ask them this question : "Why not the producer establish the price of his products as well as the manufacturer ?" Not to secure exorbitant demands, but to get a fair profit over the cost of raising the crops. No man can accumulate money who sells below cost. If you hit this point right, you will sweep the West. You must get into the farmers' pockets to reach their hearts, and a lively palpitation there invigorates their minds. I am not idle—it is not my nature, you all know ; but be yourselves active, and thus help the cause. Mark my word, there is a revolution going on among the people, and if you strike the right chord in a new circular letter you will soon see the Patrons will be a power, and yourselves at the head of them.

Fraternally yours,

O. H. KELLEY.

However, to show that the National Grange still believed in the work Mr. Kelley had set out to do and was really in hearty sympathy with him in it, the following resolution, adopted by that body, Oct. 3, 1868, may be cited :

Resolved, That we renewedly commend our beloved brother, O. H. Kelley, Secretary of the National Grange, to the kindness and confidence of our friends everywhere, as one of the earliest advocates of our Order, the most laborious worker in organizing it, and framing and harmonizing its ritual, and now indefatigable in extending its borders and strengthening its influence in the Western states, proving himself a workman in this new and important field that needeth not to be ashamed—the right man in the right place. May his success be commensurate with his diligence and perseverance, and the wide-spreading beneficence of the Order be his abundant joy and reward.

The month of July, 1868, Mr. Kelley often said was the darkest month in the history of the Order. Of this period he has written : "The eventful year closed, and the last scene in my imagination was the tableau of one struggling almost against hope, while a kind friend, like a fairy, was pointing with her finger at these words, charmingly radiant with sunset hues on fleecy clouds : 'The diligent man shall prosper; he shall stand before kings; he shall not stand before mean men.'"

It may not be amiss just here to say that Mr. Kelley, in a personal letter to the author, insisted that Miss Hall, the "kind friend" above referred to, should have greater credit than he for the success of the Grange in those early days. He says, "Had it not been for Miss Hall I should have given up the work in the second year." Beyond all question, then, she is as justly entitled to be known as one of the "founders" of the Order as anyone to whom that title has ever been given.

CHAPTER III.

Brighter Prospects.

THE early months of the year 1869 saw a rapid increase in membership in the Order in the State of Minnesota, and it seems remarkable, as we look back to those early days, that the state so sparsely settled at that time should have been really foremost in the work of organizing granges. They were established mostly in the interior, away from large villages and cities. Mr. Kelley relates how, on January 4 of that year, he went to a little place called Maple Plain, consisting of scarce a dozen houses scattered among trees and stumps. Streets there were none, but only footpaths across lots. The first meeting was held and degrees conferred in a room about 12x16 feet in dimensions, in which there was "a cook stove, bed and other furniture." Nevertheless the Grange was organized. "Maple Plain set the ball in motion in the big woods and there was no use trying to stop it." The Order continued to grow and on February 23, 1869, the State Grange of Minnesota was organized, the first in the United States, with Truman M. Smith as Master. There were 11 subordinate granges in Minnesota.

It was on the journey home that Mr. Kelley found himself in a railroad accident. Part of the train was thrown from the track, and the car in which he was seated was left with one end in the ditch and the other up in the air. He says, "I was in the up end, of course." Lucky enough ! Had he been in the down end what the newly established Order would have suffered one now dreads to contemplate.

A pleasant event occurred in April of 1869 when Mr. Kelley revisited Fredonia grange. They gave him a splendid entertainment in the evening and he found that the grange had grown to 100 members. George D. Hinckley was then Master. After paying a visit to F. M. McDowell at Wayne he went on to Washington to attend the first annual session of the National Grange, which was held on April 13, 1869. This body was not imposing in numbers but rich in experience. Those present were: Messrs. Saunders, Grosh, Ireland, Trimble, Thompson and Kelley. The report of the Secretary showed that nine dispensations were issued for 1868 and "one Grange organized gratuitous in Minnesota." A pattern of regalia was adopted in order to secure uniformity throughout the Order. It was at this meeting that Miss Hall was appointed Assistant to the Secretary "at a salary of $600 for a year." Several "laws" were adopted, none of which seem to be in existence at the present day. The Secretary was authorized to continue the work of organization, with full power to make such use of the funds he received as circumstances might require, and to adopt such plans as in his judgment would be expedient for the good of the Order."

There was considerable discussion in the Minnesota granges about this time as to appointing a general business agent of the order, and the subject was also brought before the National Grange. Minnesota was very desirous of having an agent, and in fact did appoint one, who should be responsible to the Minnesota State Grange only and not to the National. A letter from William Paist, Secretary of the Minnesota

State Grange, to Mr. Kelley, adds a humorous touch to this matter of the state agency. It is given below :

ST. PAUL, April 2d, 1869.

While sitting around Brother Prescott's stove (a quorum), we received a letter from Brother Chadbourne, approving Brother Prescott's appointment as State Agent, and requesting him to go down on Robert street and purchase a jackass for him. As this is his first order, we thought it too good to keep until you got back, and the quorum has directed me to inform you officially of it. Reports are coming in. Hurry home; we are lonesome.

WM. PAIST, Secretary State Grange.

On this was the memorandum : " This purchasing business commenced with buying jackasses ; the prospects are that many will be sold."

It was about this time that the suggestion was made that the National Grange purchase a house and lot in the vicinity of Cincinnati and make that the future home of the Order. That these early builders had still great expectations will be seen from the fact that they were discussing the matter of erecting a temple. Also of holding at Cincinnati a biennial exposition of the products of the United States, believing that on such an occasion they might bring into that city 200,000 or 300,000 visitors. But the temple was never erected and the exposition never held, and the 200,000 or 300,000 visitors never arrived there, at least not under Grange auspices.

Mr. Kelley never considered himself much of a speech maker, and the following somewhat humorous incident will illustrate his feeling on receiving an invitation to address the Kalmar Grange in Minnesota. He mentioned the matter of receiving the invitation to Mr. Thompson as a good joke as " it was something I knew myself unfitted for," he said. We relate the remainder of the incident in his own words :

"However, I had to learn all about everything connected with the Order, and following his advice, set myself at work to prepare the oration. I was not many days putting some items together that would be instructive, and setting forth the objects of the organization. Next, I commenced preparing to deliver it. The first thing was to prune it down from an hour to thirty minutes in length; then to practice in the reading and oratorical exercise. I had nearly committed it to memory, but knew very well as soon as I should rise before an audience of over twenty persons every word would fly from my mind. Hence I determined to rely upon my manuscript. One afternoon, my family being away from home, I repaired to the barn for active practice. My nearest neighbor lived half a mile away, so I felt secure from interruption, even should my stentorian lungs make the grove ring. I intended to practice for an audience of ten thousand - either a success or a failure—but whichever, it should be on a grand scale.

"On the threshing floor I had placed an empty barrel, and on that box I placed the manuscript speech I intended to empty upon the audience. I commenced reading aloud, gradually increasing my voice, until I worked myself up to a frenzy of excitement that would have made a Booth weep. The poultry, languidly scratching around the barn that summer afternoon, began to 'prick up their ears' and show indications of an appreciation of the noise, at any rate, while the old farm dog came to me, evidently in sympathy, or trying to cool down my unusual excitement; but I heeded nothing until I had finished my peroration, and was about to sit down, when immediately an old rooster, that had been eyeing me sideways for the last five minutes, clapped his wings and crowed most lustily.

"That was perhaps a good omen, but I am satisfied it was all the crowing the speech ever elicited I went to the meeting (the picnic had been abandoned); I read my remarks very tamely, and returned home well satisfied that speech-making was not my forte."

There were now all told about 50 granges in the United States.

On November 27, 1869, the first subordinate Grange in Illinois, that did any genuine work, was organized. On December 24, Honey Creek Grange No. 1 was organized in Indiana, the first in that state.

The year 1870 opened with encouragement. The meeting of the National Grange was held at Washington—its second annual session. From the report of the Secretary made at that meeting, we make the following extracts, which will summarize the work already accomplished:

"In presenting to you my second Annual Report, it gives me pleasure to say that dispensations have been issued as follows: Minnesota has forty, Illinois three, Iowa three, Pennsylvania one, New York one, Ohio one. Of this number, thirty-nine have been issued during the past year, against ten the previous year Added to this is one State Grange—that of Minnesota. While you require from me prompt reports of my doings, and take the liberty to censure any apparent delays on my part, it is but justice and courtesy, in return, that you should promptly reply to my communications. The Order has been introduced to the public under difficulties. No liberal donations have been provided from which to draw in an emergency, and the work has been up-hill business. I would call your attention to the necessity of establishing, at an early day, a newspaper at the Capitol, to be the organ of our Order, and place it under the immediate supervision of our Worthy Master. I suggest that this be done by a stock company, consisting of members of the Order. The plan of such a company is for you to devise."

Several proposed amendments to the Constitution were discussed and adopted. We call attention to but two of them as being of present interest; the one refers to the number of negative votes required to reject an applicant, increasing same from one to three; the other, which made it illegal to confer more than two degrees at the same meeting unless by virtue of a dispensation. An order of business was prepared for subordinate granges, which was essentially the same as the one in present use.

On March 2, 1870, was organized the first subordinate grange in the State of Ohio. It is interesting to note here that an effort was made to organize a Grange in New York City among the "hornyhanded" toilers of the soil in that 'burg.

Mr. Kelley now returned to his home in Minnesota after an absence of five months. During this time many letters had been received bearing on the progress of the work of organization and containing many suggestions as to advancing the interests of the Order. Among these was the suggestion that a German ritual be prepared which was done later, but no use was ever made of it. The work of selecting efficient deputies was thoroughly considered in many of these letters; also the suggestion that there be a Patron's grip with each degree.

June 10th of that year the first subordinate Grange was organized in Tennessee. On July 11th the Illinois State Grange was organized, with Daniel Worthington as Master. On August 17th, California came into the fold with its first Grange at Pilot Hill, Eldorado County, and on the 25th of the same month Missouri organized.

On December 8, 1870, Secretary Kelley issued a circular letter from Washington, whither he had gone to reside, stating that thereafter the office of the Secretary of the National Grange would be located in that city. He further said that the Order is now working in 15 states and rapidly increasing. "To secure to our members all the benefits to be derived from a fraternity so extensive as this must become," he said, "we wish to organize subordinate granges in every town in the United States," and a plan for organizing by letter was adopted. The intention was to effect only a preliminary organization by letter, until an authorized Deputy could visit the Grange and complete its organization by giving the unwritten work of the Order, but the fact was, qualified deputies were not numerous enough to follow up these preliminary organizations, and it was only a matter of time when such granges should become dormant or pass out of existence altogether. It is related that one Grange in Texas did not receive the unwritten work of the Order until six years after its organization by the "letter" method. The secret work was never communicated by letter.

It was in the year 1870 that the following circular letter was issued by the National Grange at Washington, which sets forth the organizers' purposes as well as anything that can here be presented :

It is evident to all intelligent minds that the time has come when those engaged in rural pursuits should have an organization devoted entirely to their interests. Such it is intended to make the Order of

Patrons. It was instituted in 1867; its growth is unprecedented in the history of secret associations, and it is acknowledged one of the most useful and powerful organizations in the United States. Its grand objects are not only general improvement in husbandry, but to increase the general happiness, wealth and prosperity of the country. It is founded upon the axioms that the products of the soil comprise the basis of all wealth; that individual happiness depends upon general prosperity, and that the wealth of a country depends upon the general intelligence and mental culture of the producing classes.

In the meetings of this Order, all but members are excluded, and there is in its proceedings a symbolized ritual, pleasing, beautiful and appropriate, which is designed not only to charm the fancy, but to cultivate and enlarge the mind and purify the heart, having, at the same time, strict adaptation to rural pursuits.

The secrecy of the ritual and proceedings of the Order have been adopted chiefly for the purpose of accomplishing desired efficiency, extension and unity, and to secure among its members in the internal workings of the Order, confidence, harmony and security.

Women are admitted to full membership, and we solicit the co-operation of woman, because of a conviction that without her aid success will be less certain and decided. Much might be said in this connection, but every husband and brother knows that where he can be accompanied by his wife or sister, no lessons will be learned but those of purity and truth.

The Order of the PATRONS OF HUSBANDRY will accomplish a thorough and systematic organization among Farmers and Horticulturists throughout the United States, and will secure among them intimate social relations and acquaintance with each other, for the advancement and elevation of their pursuits, with an appreciation and protection of their true interests. By such means may be accomplished that which exists throughout the country in all other avocations, and among all other classes — combined co-operative association for individual improvement and common benefit.

Among the advantages which may be derived from the Order, are systematic arrangements for procuring and disseminating, in the most expeditious manner, information relative to crops, demand and supply, prices, markets, and transportation throughout the country; also for the purchase and exchange of stock, seeds, and desired varieties of plants and trees, and for the purpose of procuring help at home or from abroad, and situations for persons seeking employment; also for ascertaining and testing the merits of newly invented farming implements, and those not in general use, and for detecting and exposing those that are unworthy, and for protecting, by all available means, the farming interests from fraud and deception, and combinations of every kind.

We ignore all political or religious discussions in the Order; we do not solicit the patronage of any sect, association or individual, upon any grounds whatever, except upon the intrinsic merits of the Order.

CHAPTER IV.

The Years 1871 and 1872.

ON January 4, 1871, the third annual meeting of the National Grange was held in Washington. The Secretary made an informal report of the work for the year and several important communications were read from subordinate granges. In one of these we find the first suggestion for a County Grange, made by C. C. Low, Master of Lincoln Grange No. 46, Gillford, Minn. Said County Grange was to be composed of Masters and Past Masters of subordinate granges, to meet semi-annually or annually, as might be determined, and to discuss any local or general questions which might properly come before the meeting. Secretary Kelley in a memorandum says that the object of this was almost exclusively to create a local corporation for buying machinery or goods and for shipping produce. There was but little else of importance done at this meeting.

On January 6, 1871, Honey Creek Grange of Indiana erected, and later dedicated, the first Grange hall in the United States, we believe, and the first attempt at co-operation was made about this time by Mr. Hinckley of Fredonia Grange. However, co-operation did not become a marked success at that time.

On January 12th the State Grange of Iowa was organized at Des Moines, with Dudley W. Adams as Master and Gen. William Duane Wilson, Secretary. On January 13th the first application for a subordinate

Grange in Wisconsin was received. On February 22, 1871, the first genuine working Grange in Pennsylvania was organized, known as Eagle Grange, No. 1, of Clinton, Pa. On May 20th, Mississippi came into the Order with its first Grange, located at Rienzi, and on the 24th of the same month Charleston, S. C., organized Ashley Grange, No. 1. On June 12th of that year Wisconsin State Grange was organized, with S. W. Pierce as Master. On July 4th the first Grange in Vermont was organized by Jonathan Lawrence; it was called Green Mountain Grange, No. 1. Next to unfurl the Grange banner was Kentucky, with Pioneer Grange, No. 1, organized by R. S. Reeves, August 10, 1871. In October of that year Secretary Kelley took a trip into New England, spending three weeks in Vermont, but did not meet with any special success in the work of organization. He said New England was the hardest to interest in the work of any section. On the 27th of December, the first dispensation for New Jersey was issued for Homestead Grange, No. 1. Mortimer Whitehead, later a lecturer of the National Grange, was a charter member of Homestead Grange.

The fourth annual session of the National Grange was held at Washington on January 3, 1872, and Secretary Kelley's report at that time summarizes the work thus far accomplished. We quote from his report:

"In February, 1868, there was but one Subordinate Grange in the United States; this I left in good working order in April of that year. On my return the following year, I reported ten Subordinates and one State Grange for the year's work. In 1869, there were organized thirty nine Subordinates and one State Grange. In 1870, there were organized thirty-eight Subordinates and one State Grange, and in 1871, there have been one hundred and thirty Subordinates organized. * * * * The educational and social features of our Order offer inducement to some to join, but the majority desire pecuniary benefits—advantages in purchase of machinery and sales of produce. To bring all the Granges into direct communication, and to devise a system of co-

JOHN TRIMBLE.

operation, devolves upon the National Grange. But until its membership is much increased, we must wait patiently the appearance of our new Moses, who is to present the coveted plan. * * * * In conclusion, we see what the Order is today. Its future depends upon our action. Though we are few in number, we can exert our influence. For my own part, I have been left by you to labor as I have thought best, I might almost say "solitary and alone," yet all will acknowledge my faith in the ultimate success of the Order. If I have made mistakes at times, none of them have been serious or irreparable.

Considerable business was transacted at this meeting of the National Grange relative to the secret work, charters, deputies, dues, etc. The Treasurer, Mr. Ireland, having tendered his resignation, J. R. Thompson was elected to fill the vacancy, which consequently made a vacancy in the office of Lecturer. This was filled by the appointment of D. W. Adams of Iowa. On January 1, he organized the first Grange in that state, namely Harlan County Grange, No. 1, and on the 10th of January, Michigan enrolled its first Grange as Burnside Grange, No. 1. Virginia came next with her first Grange at Petersburg, on February 16, and far off Oregon presented an application dated January 6th. It had 30 charter members. The State Grange of Indiana was organized March 1, 1872, with John Weir as Master, and on the 5th day of March the State Grange of Illinois was reorganized, the first organization having been annuled, as nothing had been done by the officers to advance the Order in that state. Alonzo Golder was elected Master. Mississippi State Grange was organized on March 15th, with Gen. A. J. Vaughan as Master, and on the same date Louisiana asked for membership in the Order with its first Subordinate Grange. In January of that year 54 new granges had been organized. February closed with 82 and March had nearly 100.

On April 2d, application was received for the first Subordinate Grange in Kansas, which was called Hiawatha Grange, No. 1, and had 44 charter members. The month of April showed 98 new granges.

The record for May seems to be wanting, but June closed with 86 new dispensations. It was on July 3, 1872, that the State Grange of Vermont was organized at St. Johnsbury, with E. P. Colton as Master and C. J. Bell, at present (1904) Master of the State Grange and Secretary of the National Grange Executive Committee and Governor of the State of Vermont, was elected Treasurer of the organization. On August 2d, the State Grange of Nebraska was organized, with William P. Porter as Master, and on August 3d Arkansas came into the fold with its first grange, organized at Phillips Academy by Hon. J. T. Jones. The next was Canada, which put in its first application on August 16th. The first grange was organized by Eben Thompson. Georgia organized Valdosta Grange, No. 1, on October 2d.

On December 9, the State Grange of Kansas was organized, with F. H. Dumbauld as Master. The month closed with 120 new granges, making a total for the year of 1105. Secretary Kelley says, "It may be presumed the close of the year found all of my family in fine spirits. Our united efforts for five years, the hard labor and many privations all were rewarded by success."

CHAPTER V.

Permanent Organization Effected.

A NEW Era began with the permanent organization of a National Grange, in the early days of 1873, at Georgetown, D. C. With this meeting the work of Secretary Kelley and Miss Hall virtually closed. They passed the temporary organization over to the incorporated body, free of debt, except what was due to themselves, and with cash enough on hand to defray the general expenses of the session. Secretary Kelley made his financial report and from it we glean the following facts: There were organized, during the year 1872, 1105 new granges, the fees for dispensations for which amounted to $16,375. Iowa reported 652 new granges in that year; the total receipts, according to the treasurer's report, were $17,768.51. There were issued 1,705,000 sheets of printed matter for gratuitous distribution almost entirely. That year State Granges were organized in eight states, i. e., Illinois (reorganized), Indiana, Wisconsin (reorganized), Vermont, South Carolina, Nebraska, Mississippi and Kansas. To anticipate the record a little, we give here the State Granges that were organized during 1873, which were as follows: Alabama, Arkansas, California, Dakota, Florida, Georgia, Kentucky, Louisiana, Massachusetts, Michigan, Missouri, New Hampshire, New Jersey, New York, North Carolina, Ohio, Oregon, Pennsylvania, Tennessee, Texas, Virginia, West Virginia. In 1874 came Colorado, Maine, Maryland and Montana. Iowa took the lead in the number of granges, i. e., 754 and South Carolina came next with 102. Mississippi had 61. There were subordinate granges in 22 states and three in Canada, the total number being 1362.

It was at this session of the National Grange that the Constitution and By-Laws were adopted which were essentially the same as those which at present govern the Order. The election of officers took place with the following result:

Master—Dudley W. Adams, Waukon, Iowa.
Overseer—Thomas Taylor, Columbia, S. C.
Lecturer—T. A. Thompson, Plainview, Minn.
Steward—A. J. Vaughan, Early Grove, Miss.
Assistant Steward—G. W. Thompson, New Brunswick, N. J.
Chaplain—A. B. Grosh, Washington, D. C.
Treasurer—F. M. McDowell, Wayne, N. Y.
Secretary—O. H. Kelley, Washington, D. C.
Gate Keeper—O. Dinwiddie, Orchard Grove, Ind.
Ceres, Mrs. D. W. Adams, Waukon, Iowa.
Pomona—Mrs. O. H. Kelley, Washington, D. C.
Flora—Mrs. J. C. Abbott, Clarkesville, Iowa.
Lady Assistant Steward, Miss C. A. Hall, Washington, D. C.
Executive Committee—William Saunders, Washington, D. C.; D. Wyatt Aiken, Cokesbury, S. C.; E. R. Shankland, Dubuque, Iowa.

Another important matter accomplished at this session was the adoption of the report on the incorporation of the Order. It was later incorporated under the laws of the State of Kentucky when the National Grange headquarters were removed to Louisville in 1876. The certificate of incorporation follows;

CERTIFICATE OF INCORPORATION.

OF THE

NATIONAL GRANGE OF THE PATRONS OF HUSBANDRY.

BE IT KNOWN, That William Saunders, O. H. Kelley, John R. Thompson, A. B. Grosh and John Trimble, Jr., of the city and county, of Washington, District of Columbia; F. M. McDowell, of Wayne

Steuben county, and State of New York; Dudley W. Adams, of Waukon, Alamakee county and State of Iowa; D. A. Robertson, of St. Paul, Ramsay county, State of Minnesota, and D. Wyatt Aiken, of Cokesbury, Abbeville county, State of South Carolina, for themselves, their associates and successors in office, being desirous of availing themselves of the provisions of the act of Congress approved May 5, 1870. entitled, "An act to provide for the creation of corporations in the District of Columbia," hereby constitute themselves, their associates and successors in office, a body politic and corporate, under the name and style of

"THE NATIONAL GRANGE OF THE PATRONS OF HUSBANDRY."

The object of this association is to act as the governing body of the Order known as "The Patrons of Husbandry," which Order is an organization among farmers and those engaged in kindred pursuits in the United States, to secure to them the advantages of co-operation in all things affecting their interests, and of mutual improvement. The following members are named as the present executive officers of the National Grange hereby incorporated: William Saunders, Master; O. H. Kelley, secretary; J. R. Thompson, Treasurer, and William Saunders, A. B. Grosh, J. R. Thompson, John Trimble, Jr., and F M. McDowell as directors or managers, known as "The Executive Committee." The corporation hereby created is to continue in existence for the period of twenty years from the date hereof.

Done and subscribed at Georgetown, District of Columbia, this tenth day of January, A. D., 1873.

WILLIAM SAUNDERS.   DUDLEY W. ADAMS.
O. H. KELLEY.   D. WYATT AIKEN.
J. R. THOMPSON.   D. A. ROBERTSON.
A. B. GROSH.   JOHN TRIMBLE, JR.
F. M. McDOWELL.

Signed in the presence of—
WM. DUANE WILSON, ALONZO GOLDER.

Properly acknowledged, before sealed, by Wilson N. Fuller, a notary public for the District of Columbia, and recorded in liber "Deeds of Incorporation, D. C.," folio 258.

Thus the Order of Patrons of Husbandry became an incorporated association and, in fact, a new Order with new Constitution and new officers. "On January 11th," says Mr. Kelley, "we closed our work and the National Grange was a reality."

CHAPTER VI.

An Unparalleled Growth.

THE annual session of the National Grange, in 1874, was held at St. Louis, Mo. The Order was now growing with unparalleled rapidity. The years 1873 and 1874 were record years for new granges, and membership was increasing with leaps and bounds. Look at Missouri! In 1873 that state had 1500 live, active, working subordinate granges within its borders. They were in nearly every one of its 114 counties and the work was spreading like wild fire. All through the land granges were springing up like mushrooms of a night. The work of organization was such as to excite the constant wonder of even the members of the Order, while those outside its gates looked on with undisguised amazement. At the sixth annual session of the National Grange nine states were represented, having within their limits 1300 subordinate granges. One year later thirty-two states and two territories were represented by regularly elected delegates who claimed jurisdiction over more than 10,000 subordinate granges. During that year 24 State Granges were organized and there were 1,294 state deputies in the field.

The address of National Master D. W. Adams at the seventh annual meeting of the National Grange contained one or two paragraphs quite as applicable to grange work of the present day as then. He said: "There is danger that, in grappling with the gigantic questions of the hour, we may lose sight of the rock upon which we builded. It is of prime importance, in order to maintain the strength of the national organization, that the subordinate granges be kept up to a high standard of efficiency. During the first months of the existence of a grange, the novelty, preparation of regalia, and initiation of new members secures a full and interested attendance. After this, there is often a want of amusing and instructive exercises, the interest flags, the attendance falls off, and the grange seems to lack vitality." Again he referred to the ofttimes perplexing question, as many granges find it, of eligibility to membership in the Order. Any person interested in "agricultural pursuits" said the Constitution. But the clause was capable of such varied interpretations that much confusion and misunderstanding resulted. And not only this but herein may be found the reason for the woeful decline in grange membership which followed a little later on and when so many granges went out of existence. Worthy Master Adams said: "To be a Patron of Husbandry is no longer of doubtful propriety, but the proudest in the land are knocking at our door. The Order has become recognized as one of the great powers in the land, and the gates are besieged, from ocean to ocean, by hordes of speculators, demagogues, small politicians, grain buyers, cotton factors, and lawyers, who suddenly discover that they are 'interested in agricultural pursuits'; but only as a hawk is interested in the sparrow. You would do well to give this matter a most careful review, and by law determine the proper construction of the constitution, so we may be able to keep our gates closed against those whose only interest consists in what they can make out of us. To have such admitted to our counsels can only result in evil, and sow seeds of internal strife."

While the Constitution is now more stringent on

this point of eligibility to membership the fact is, it is variously interpreted still, and in many granges it is so liberally interpreted that the most unfortunate results follow.

It was at this session of the National Grange that the "Declaration of Purposes" was adopted. This masterly document was from the pen of Mr. J. W. A. Wright, then of California. It stands to-day as the wisest and strongest statement of the purposes for which the grange was organized, that has ever been formulated. It should be placed in the hands of every candidate for admission to the Order, and its frequent reading in grange meetings cannot help giving members more exalted views as to the real purposes for which this Order was established.

The next National Grange meeting was held at Louisville, Ky., Nov. 17, 1875, Worthy Master Dudley W. Adams, presiding. The address of welcome given by Worthy Master Davie of the Kentucky State Grange brings out the interesting fact that there were at that time 100,000 good and true members of the Order in that state. Worthy Master Adams remarked, in his annual address, that over 2,000 subordinate granges had been organized the previous year, and remarking on the wonderful growth of the Order, Secretary Kelley said : "In the history of organization our Order is the greatest achievement of modern times. The Masonic Order, including blue lodges, chapters and commandaries, numbers, all together, 12,930 bodies. The Odd Fellows number 7,051 lodges, encampments, etc., while after eight years' growth the Order of the Patrons of Husbandry has issued 24,290 charters in the United States alone. During the year 1874 there were over 3,000 deputies at work organizing granges. Up to this date only 686 subordinate granges had been consolidated or suspended or had charters revoked since the Order was first organized. The total paying membership as reported at this, the 9th session of the National Grange, was 762.263. The total amount of monies received at the Secretary's office during the three years immediately preceding 1875 was, in round numbers, $350,000. Indiana was now the banner state, having received 2,036 charters."

These were halcyon days for the Order. The treasury was plethoric. Fees for dispensations were rolling in with every mail. The grange was on the high tide of prosperity, viewed from a financial standpoint. The National body could "do things," for did they not have the money to do with? For several years 30,000 copies of the Proceedings of each annual meeting were distributed among the subordinate granges. Miss Hall compiled a song book for the Order, for which she was given $1000 by the National Grange. The Executive Committee, desiring to aid the unlettered Masters of subordinate granges in their decisions as presiding officers, endeavored to purchase the copyright of Cushing's Manual in order that every Master might be presented with one, but failing in this, they compiled a "Patrons' Parliamentary Guide" and circulated 50,000 copies among the subordinate granges. In the paraphernalia sent out by the National Grange Secretary to each new grange was a small pruning knife, but when so many knives were required the Executive Committee visited the largest cutlery establishment in the United States and asked for a price on 10,000 knives. "Gentlemen," exclaimed the manufacturer, "do you deal in anything but knives?"

In view of the fact that the total grange membership in the United States was, on January 1, 1875, about what it is now (1904) it may be interesting to note in comparison which were the strongest grange states at that time, both North and South. It will doubtless surprise the younger members of the Order to-day that the Southern States at that time had the bulk of the membership. For instance, Alabama 17,440, Arkansas 20,471, Georgia 17,826, Florida 3,804, Kentucky 52,463, Louisiana 10,078, Maryland 5,635, Mississippi 30,797, Missouri 80,059, North Carolina 10,166, South Carolina 10,922, Tennessee 37,581, Texas 37,619, Virginia 13,885, West Virginia 5,990. The Northern States having the largest membership were Illinois 29,063, Indiana 60,298, Iowa 51,832, Kansas 40,261, Michigan 33,196, Minnesota 16,617, New York 11,723 (1904 approximately 60,000), Ohio 53,327, Pennsylvania 22,471, Wisconsin 17,226, Vermont 10,193, the other states having membership running down to about 400.

It was at this session of the National Grange that the committee reported on the Form of Dedication for grange halls, the committee reporting that the Order was indebted to the pen of Brother J. R. Thompson for this long-needed and well-supplied addition to the ritual. We find in the record for one day in the 1875 session the following memorandum: "Brother Hinckley, in behalf of the Knickerbocker Grange, No. 154, New York City, presented to the National Grange a handsomely bound Bible to lay upon its altar. The present was accepted with the thanks of the National Grange." This brings out the interesting fact that there were in New York City men and women who were "interested in agricultural pursuits" and therefore eligible to membership in the Patrons of Husbandry. But the New York City grange was short-lived of necessity. It was composed of 45 members, all wealthy men, among whom were bank presidents, sewing machine manufacturers and Wall street speculators. We are reminded also that in the previous year there had been some trouble with the grange organized in Boston, Mass. It seems that the Boston grange was organized in 1873 and was composed of a class "commonly known as middlemen." It appears from a report of the committee, considered at a later day in the session, that these "undesirable" members were grain dealers, commission men, a reporter, an editor of a business paper, and the only man connected with the farm in any way was the Lecturer of the grange. The Worthy Master issued a revocation to the Boston grange, and it appears that no official notice was taken of this demand. The result was that the National Grange recommended that the Secretary be instructed to notify all other granges that the Boston grange was no longer connected with the Patrons of Husbandry.

It was at this session of the National Grange that William Saunders, one of the founders of the Order, severed his official connection with the National Grange, his reason for the act being that he did not approve of the removal of the headquarters of the National Grange from Washington to Louisville. The Committee on Foreign Relations said that prior to February 4, 1874, 11 subordinate granges had been organized in Canada by the Deputy of the National Grange and that 15 subordinate granges had been organized since the above date without authority. When these subordinate granges were organized representations were made that the Canada granges would have an organization separate from and independent of the National Grange. Relying on these representations the Patrons in Canada, on June 2, 1874, organized the Dominion Grange of Canada, which was founded mainly on the Constitution, By-Laws, Rules and Regulations of the National Grange. The Dominion Grange increased rapidly in membership and had then about 250 sub ordinate bodies.

CHAPTER VII.

Achievements of the Grange.

HAVING thus far considered the origin and early history of the grange somewhat in detail for the first ten or fifteen years of its existence, the author's purpose, in so far, has been accomplished. Let us now look at some of the achievements of the grange in these later years.

Among the first of the important acts of legislation secured through the influence of the grange was the establishment of a Bureau of Agriculture, to be presided over by a cabinet officer known as the Secretary of Agriculture. The first resolution we find recorded in the proceedings of the National Grange was one introduced by Mr. M. D. Davie of Kentucky, at the session of the National Grange held in Chicago, Ill., in 1876, which is given below:

"Resolved, That American agriculturists demand that they shall be recognized as a real factor in this government by the establishment of a bureau of agriculture, to be presided over by a cabinet officer, who shall organize the same on a plan to be devised by the wisdom of Congress, which shall embrace, to the fullest, the agricultural interests of 20,000,000 of the people, and whose counsel and advice shall have due weight according to the same on matters affecting the agricultural people and, also, our public affairs generally."

Similar resolutions were adopted at various succeeding meetings of the National Grange, and committees were appointed to see that the legislation desired was secured. To show how persistently this battle was fought, the following brief review of the history of the bill will be of interest and may be taken as a fair sample of the efforts required to secure Congressional legislation in the farmers' behalf: The bill for the elevation of the Department of Agriculture met with serious opposition from the chairman of the committee on agriculture, but Brother D. W. Aiken of South Carolina, a member of that committee, in the third session of the 46th Congress, February 7, 1881, secured 164 votes in its favor, there being 83 against and 45 not voting, thus failing by one vote to receive the necessary two-thirds. The bill was opposed by some for the reason that it was "legislation for the protection of special interests." Another said: "We have here the spectacle of a large class of people, already strong in material resources and abundantly able to protect their own interests, clamoring for the elevation of this department and for the dispensing of special favors to them. The request is not made by the real agriculturists of the country nor by any relatively large number of intelligent men engaged in that business throughout the land." One gentleman said there was no constitutional warrant for the elevation of the Department of Agriculture or even of the establishment of the Department as it stands to-day, but that it was "the illegitimate child of the government, deserving support only during its infancy and while the act of creating it remained unrepealed." In reply to this statement Congressman Hatch said: "If this department is an illegitimate child then, in the name of the great agricultural interests of the country, let the 46th Congress of the United States do the greatest act of its official life and legitimatize this child of agriculture. Illegitimate! If it be so, it has done more for the country than any other child that has been born to it since the Declaration of Independence. It is the foundation of our wealth, the corner stone of our prosperity and the fruitful source from which we derive our richest, surest revenues."

In the first session of the 47th Congress, after a full discussion, on May 10, 1882, the House passed the Department of Agriculture bill by the overwhelming vote of 183 ayes to 7 noes, 101 not voting. In the 48th Congress, December 15, 1884, the bill again passed the House by the decisive vote of 166 ayes to 69 noes, 88 not voting. In the 49th Congress, January 11, 1887, after mature deliberation and discussion by the House, the bill was passed by the overwhelming vote of 226 ayes to 26 noes, 67 not voting. On February 23, 1887, the bill, with amendments, passed the Senate, was returned to the House the next day, was referred to the committee on agriculture and the following day was reported back to the House with the recommendation that the said amendment be concurred in. Owing to a lack of time before adjournment of the 49th Congress, it was impossible to obtain consideration of the Senate amendment by the House and the measure again failed to become a law. The principal amendment placed upon the bill by the Senate in the closing days of the 49th Congress was to the effect that the weather service of the United States Signal Service Bureau should be transferred to the Department of Agriculture. The amendment was approved by the House. At the next session of Congress, March 7, 1888, the committee on agriculture reported the bill to the House with the section intact and without alteration, and it was thus passed by the House on May 21st and again sent to the Senate. There it was not acted upon until September 21, 1888, when it was returned to the House with amendments, the only one of importance being to strike out the fifth section which had originated in the Senate and had been accepted by the House. The Senate committee kept the bill four months and, finding no other pretext for preventing its passing at that session, deliberately struck out the section of the bill which had originated in the Senate at the last session and which was deemed of value and importance by the farmers of America. But justice finally triumphed, and in 1899 National Master J. H. Brigham, in his annual address to the National Grange, said that for several years they had tried to secure the elevation of the Department of Agriculture but the repeated failures had not discouraged them. "It is my privilege, at this session," said he, "to report that our perseverance has been rewarded and the chief of the Department of Agriculture will henceforth be a trusted adviser to the President." Thus, after 12 years of unremitting endeavor, the grange won one of its most notable victories for the farmers of the United States.

I have given the history of this measure thus in detail to show the obstacles that the National Grange had to overcome in its attempt to secure this legislation, now acknowledged to have been most wise and most beneficial to the agricultural interests of the United States.

Among other achievements of the grange of national importance may be mentioned the law, passed through its influence, preventing the renewal of patents on sewing machines, which saved many million dollars to purchasers annually by reducing the cost fully 50 per cent. Through legislation instituted by the grange, transportation companies were brought under legislative control, and out of this agitation came the decision of the Supreme Court of the United States that "a creature cannot be greater than the creator; i. e., corporations must be subject to governmental control." The Inter-State Commerce Commission law was also enacted largely through the influence of the grange, and the anti-oleomargarine legislation which required oleomargarine and butterine to be branded.

and sold as such, and not palmed off on the consumer as butter, was brought about by the assistance of the grange legislative committee and representatives of dairy interests. The establishment of Experiment Stations in many states was the direct outcome of persistent grange endeavor, and reforms in ballot laws were made possible in certain states because the grange demanded them. Among the other enactments of Congress which the grange was largely influential in procuring, were the so-called Sherman Anti-Trust Law of 1890 and the various amendments since that time adopted; the law adopted in 1903 creating the Department of Commerce; the separation of agricultural schools from the classical colleges and the Act of 1902 preventing the false branding of food products thus protecting farmers from fraudulent imitations, and consumers from the imposition of fraudulent imitations being sold to them as pure articles.

Perhaps no achievement of the grange has more directly benefitted the rural population than the free delivery of rural mail. And its benefits are still being extended by increasing the number of free mail routes all over the country as the government increases its appropriations therefor. After several years' discussion in the subordinate granges, in 1894 the National Grange took action and sent a committee to Washington, asking Congress to investigate the subject, and if found practicable to adopt it, and at that time an appropriation of $10,000 was made by Congress to experiment in delivering mail at farmers' homes. This experiment met with opposition on every hand, from postmasters, merchants, and members of Congress, until 1897, when the appropriation for this service was stricken from the postoffice appropriation bill by the Senate. The Legislative Committee of the National Grange went to Washington and had a conference with leading senators; the opposition was withdrawn, the appropriation made and the extension of this system has continued ever since, and will go on until, so far as is practical, every rural home will have free delivery of mail. If the Order had never secured anything through national legislation except the free delivery of rural mail, this alone would more than justify its existence. The introduction of this service has proceeded with marvelous rapidity. At the beginning of the fiscal year 1899, says a government report, there were less than 200 routes in operation. At the close of the present year (1904) the number in actual operation will be in excess of 25,000, bringing a daily mail service to more than 12,500,000 of our people residing in the rural districts. At the present time complete service is established in 142 counties, in which all the people outside of the cities receive their mail daily by rural free delivery carriers.

The policy of rural free delivery is no longer a subject of serious dispute. It has unmistakably vindicated itself by its fruits. The practical benefits and the popular appreciation and demand have been decisively demonstrated. It has been made plain that this service is a potent educational force; that it brings agricultural life into far closer relations with the active business world; that it keeps the farmers in daily touch with markets and prices; that it advances general intelligence through the increased circulation of legitimate journals and periodicals, stimulates correspondence, quickens all interchanges, promotes good roads, enhances farm values, makes farm life less isolated and more attractive, and unites with other wholesome influences in checking and changing the hitherto prevailing current from country to city. The national value of these advantages is incalculable. The appropriation made by the present Congress (1904) for the continuation of the service and its extension into districts where its introduction is justifiable was $20,816,600.

Hon. Aaron Jones in his annual address to the National Grange at its meeting in Portland, Oregon, in November 1904, said: "A generation has passed, crowded with greater advancement than any similar period in the world's history, since our organization was founded to meet conditions essential to public welfare. It was consecrated to develop the best type of social conditions, to foster and promote good citizenship, to develop agriculture, to secure equity in the business relations of the agricultural classes with the industrial and commercial interests of our country. It has gone steadily forward on its mission, its standard has been held high, by clean hands and honest hearts of good men and women, devoted to principle, above sordid and selfish ambitions. We contemplate its glorious record of usefulness and beneficence with emotions of thankfulness and pride. No pen can fully describe, no words of mine can picture the thrilling joys, the happy emotions inspired and promoted in the hearts and in the happy homes in the hundreds of thousands of its members scattered throughout our country. The grange removed the isolation of farm homes, inculcated and promoted education, fostered and secured better schools for our children, raised the standard of intelligence among the farming population, developed the latent talent of its members, making them logical thinkers and writers and fluent speakers, understanding the relation of agriculture to the varied and complex social, industrial and commercial interests of our country and the world. These glorious results were attained by steadfast adherence to the principles of our Order and methods suggested by the founders of our Fraternity."

In a hundred ways state and local measures relative to good roads, libraries, reading rooms, banks, fire insurance companies, co-operative enterprises, trade systems, etc., have found in the grange their most efficient advocates. It should be further borne in mind that the influence of the grange has been an important factor in preventing much legislation that would have worked injury to agricultural interests.

Likewise has the grange been influential in the work along social and educational lines. By precept and practice it has ever striven to promote intelligence, improve society, elevate citizenship, better rural conditions and develop "a better and higher manhood and womanhood among ourselves," mutually resolving "to labor for the good of the Order, our Country and Mankind." What the grange has accomplished in its attempt to fulfill that purpose shall not be fully known or portrayed "until the day when the books are opened and the record of each is read."

A FORWARD LOOK.

" *Yesterday, To-day, To-morrow,*
These three—
But the greatest of these
Is To-morrow."

Grand as have been the achievements of the grange in the Past and wonderful as has been its progress; powerful, aggressive and influential as it is To-day, as under its banner are marshaled the Patron hosts, yet all that it has done, or is now doing, is but a foregleam of what, under wise guidance, it may do and be in the To-morrow of its history as it goes forward on its God-given mission, elevating humanity, developing manhood and womanhood, and carrying a broader culture into agricultural life.

In governmental legislation, in the farmer's behalf, there is an ever-widening field of duty and opportunity. Not yet has the farmer come fully into the enjoyment of his political birthright. Not yet has he taken his rightful position in the affairs of state and the councils of the nation. Not yet has the Goddess of Agriculture been laurel-crowned! Vast and intricate problems touching labor, taxation, transportation, oppressive combinations and the like, are to be solved in the coming years, and these bear most directly on the welfare of the farmer as a tiller of the soil and the producer of a world's necessities. Likewise in state and local legislation there are questions in which the agriculturist will find himself most vitally interested and in the just and equitable determination of which the grange must bear its part, exerting its influence and power conservatively, wisely but effectually. In the work of educating its members along such lines of thought and action as shall make them true citizens, with lofty ideals and noble aspirations, the grange shall find one of its grandest opportunities. And the silver thread of secrecy, running through the fabric of our Fraternity, shall bind into one great, strong, influential organization a happy, prosperous, agricultural people—Patrons of Husbandry, indeed,—in whose sacred circle "unbounded confidence prevails, and where the welfare of each is bound up in the good of all."

"For the structure that we raise,
  Time is with materials filled;
Our To-days and Yesterdays
  Are the blocks with which we build.

Build To-day, then, strong and sure,
  With a firm and ample base;
And ascending and secure
  Shall To-morrow find its place."

ANNUAL SESSIONS OF THE NATIONAL GRANGE.

YEAR.	PLACE.	MASTER.
1873	Washington, D. C.	William Saunders
1874	St. Louis, Missouri	Dudley W. Adams
1875	Louisville, Kentucky	Dudley W. Adams
1876	Chicago, Illinois	John T. Jones
1877	Cincinnati, Ohio	John T. Jones
1878	Richmond, Virginia	Samuel E. Adams
1879	Canandaigua, N. Y.	Samuel E. Adams
1880	Washington, D. C.	J. J. Woodman
1881	Washington, D. C.	J. J. Woodman
1882	Indianapolis, Indiana	J. J. Woodman
1883	Washington, D. C.	J. J. Woodman
1884	Nashville, Tennessee	J. J. Woodman
1885	Boston, Massachusetts	Put Darden
1886	Philadelphia, Pennsylvania	Put Darden
1887	Lansing, Michigan	James Draper
1888	Topeka, Kansas	J. H. Brigham
1889	Sacramento, California	J. H. Rrigham
1890	Atlanta, Georgia	J. H. Brigham
1891	Springfield, Ohio	J. H. Brigham
1892	Concord, New Hampshire	J. H. Brigham
1893	Syracuse, New York	J. H. Brigham
1894	Springfield, Illinois	J. H. Brigham
1895	Worcester, Massachusetts	J. H. Brigham
1896	Washington, D. C.	J. H. Brigham
1897	Harrisburg, Pennsylvania	Aaron Jones
1898	Concord, New Hampshire	Aaron Jones
1899	Springfield, Ohio	Aaron Jones
1900	Washington, D. C.	Aaron Jones
1901	Lewiston, Maine	Aaron Jones
1902	Lansing, Michigan	Aaron Jones
1903	Rochester, New York	Aaron Jones
1904	Portland, Oregon	Aaron Jones
1905	Atlantic City, New Jersey	Aaron Jones
1906	Denver, Colorado	N. J. Bachelder
1907	Hartford, Connecticut	N. J. Bachelder
1908	Washington, D. C.	N. J. Bachelder
1909	Des Moines, Iowa	N. J. Bachelder
1910	Atlantic City, New Jersey	N. J. Bachelder
1911	Columbus, Ohio	N. J. Bachelder

APPENDIX

Rise of the Granger Movement

From the Popular Science Monthly December 1887
BY CHARLES W. PIERSON

In 1866, one O. H. Kelley, a clerk in the Agricultural Department, was sent by the Commissioner of Agriculture on a tour of inspection through some of the Southern States. Impressed with the demoralization of the farming population, he hit upon the idea of organization for social and educational purposes, as a means for these people to better their condition. An ardent Mason, he naturally thought of an organization similar to the Masonic, in whose ritual, secrecy and fraternity he saw the secret of that permanence which all agricultural societies had failed to attain. A niece in Boston, to whom he first mentioned the idea, recommended that women be given membership, thus originating an important feature. On returning to Washington, Kelley took six other immortals into his confidence, and the seven set about developing the plan and constructing a ritual. It would be a long story to tell how, by two years' labor in the intervals of their regular work, they constructed a constitution providing for a national, state, county and district organization, and a ritual with seven degrees; how the names—Patrons of Husbandry for the body in general and Granges for the subordinate chapters—were finally hit upon, the latter being taken, not on account of its etymological meaning (Latin granum), but from the name of a recent novel. Suffice it to say that on December 4, 1867, a day still celebrated as the birthday of the order, the seven assembled, and, with an assurance almost sublime, solemnly organized themselves as the "National Grange of the Patrons of Husbandry." There was none to dispute the title, and they enjoyed it alone for the next five years. It is hard to tell just what were the expectations of these men. Kelley has been called everything from an unselfish philanthropist to a scheming adventurer. One can not but admire the pluck with which he perservered through great discouragements, and the unselfish spirit in which he and his fellow-workers surrendered control of the movement when it had become a power in the land. Their first step was to organize a mock Grange among their fellow clerks and their wives, to experiment with the ritual. The experiment proving satisfactory, Kelley resigned his clerkship and started out to proclaim the Grange to the world, armed only with a few dollars, and a sort of introductory letter from the other six to mankind at large.

He was not a success as a lecturer. Moreover, he made the mistake of laboring in the larger towns, instead of in the country. The four or five Granges that he coaxed into life at once preceeded to die, and he finally reached Minnesota penniless, but not discouraged. Even while the six at Washington were becoming faint-hearted, and writing to him that the landlady was pressing them grieviously for hall-rent, and that it would be wise to give up the whole business, he could issue a circular dilating upon the success of the order and the distinguished agriculturists at Washington who founded it. At his home near Itasca, he worked on furiously * * * till finally signs of success began to appear. He had organized a few Granges in Minnesota and was able to deteet a growing interest in other states. The prime necessity now was to encourage this feeble beginning, and by all means to keep it under the delusion that it was part of a powerful national organization. To this end every cent that could be earned or borrowed was used in distributing photographs of the founders, along with a mass of circulars and documents purporting to come from the national office at Washington. Every important question was ostensibly referred by Kelley to the Executive Committee at the same place, and the decisions and power of this mythical body were held in great awe by the Patrons. But other men were becoming interested and going to work. In Minnesota they were able to organize a State Grange, having mustered the fifteen district Granges required by the constitution. Two years later the State Grange of Iowa was organized, and its Worthy Master crossed the country to attend what the founders were pleased to call the "Fifth Annual Session of the National Grange." He was the first member of the order to meet with the seven. What he thought on ascertaining the real state of things is not recorded. However, he did not give up the work, and later he became Worthy Master of the National Grange. The order kept growing. At the sixth annual session, held at Georgetown in January, 1873, there were delegates from eleven states, and four women were present; 1,074 Granges had been organized during the year. The founders now gave up their offices, not even reserving the right to vote, and delivered over the results of six years' labor to their successors. For the first time, the greatest of farmers' societies was in the hands of farmers.

WONDERFUL GRANGE GROWTH.

The next two years were years of astounding development and growth—a growth almost unparalleled in the history of secret organizations, and resembling that of the Know-Nothings twenty years before. At the end of 1872 about 1,300 Granges had been organized. In the year 1873, 8,668 more were added; and in 1874, 11,941, making a total of almost 22,000, with an average membership of forty. Some idea of the magnitude of these figures may be gained from the fact that the whole number of lodges of Masons and Odd Fellows in the world was estimated at about 20,000. The order was represented in every state except Rhode Island. It had been established in the Indian Territory, whence it appealed for help to the National Grange because the governor of the Chickasaw nation looked on it with suspicion, and had ordered all Grangers out of the Chickasaw country. It had taken root in Canada, where, a few years later, there were 860 subordinate Granges. One deputy introduced it into England; others were laboring in France and Germany; and inquiries and invitations were coming even from Australia and Tasmania.

Grange treasuries were overflowing. In 1873 and 1874 the dues to the National Grange alone, according to the official statement, amounted to $348,532.20. The press was discussing the new order with alarm. Legislative committees were scurrying about the country to see what could be done for the farmer. In the words of the New York "Nation", "the farmer was the spoiled child of our politics." The House of Representatives at Washington was overawed at the new power that was apparently rising in politics, and those who claimed, for the most part falsely, to represent the movement enjoyed an astonishing influence. Among other legislation secured by these men, one bill was rushed through for printing and distributing to the farmers certain agricultural documents, at an expense of $500,000! W. W. Phelps opposed it, only to be bitterly attacked on the score of sympathy with monopolists and lack of sympathy with farmers. One fervid orator from Kansas went over his whole record for proof of this, and alleged many damaging facts—among them that he was rich, that he was interested in banks and railroads, and that he had been graduated with honor from Yale College. "These Grangers," exclaimed the orator, "mean business; . . . they are chosen to be the sovereigns of the mightiest republic of earth." Various cities strove for the honor of having the National Grange offices located within their limits, one offering to give a splendid building, another to furnish necessary officeroom and an annuity of $5,000 for five years, but the Grange was rich and independent in those days. At the seventh annual session held at St. Louis in 1874, a declaration of purposes was adopted which still remains the official statement.

The Grange had now reached the zenith of its power. One year later, in the stormy meeting held at Charleston, measure was passed for the distribution of the surplus revenue of the National Grange which may be said to mark the beginning of Grange decadence. But a consideration of this decadence may well be postponed for a time. Any discussion of the causes of the Grange's astonishing growth has been deferred to this point, in order that they may be considered in connection with the railroad legislation of the early seventies, with which the Grange, to most minds, is so entangled.

THE GRANGER MOVEMENT.

In everything published on the subject, the anti-railroad movement is called the Granger movement; the resulting legislation, the Granger legislation; the cases that arose, the Granger cases. It must be granted that the same farmers often were engaged in the "Farmers' Movement", and that certain subordinate parts of the Grange did sometimes disobey their organic law so far as to engage as bodies in the agitation, chiefly by memorializing Legislatures. It was impossible to control completely the rank and file of such a vast order. But, with these reservations, the Grange, as an organization, took no part in the anti-railroad agitation. The two were not cause and effect, but parallel effects of the same general causes. In the way of proof the "Declaration of Purposes" of 1874 has been quoted, to the effect that the Grange is not hostile to railroads, and that all political action and discussion is totally excluded. The published proceedings of the National Grange show the same thing. In 1874 the executive committee reported: "Unfortunately for the order, the impression prevails to some extent that its chief mission is to fight railroads." In 1875 a resolution from Texas favoring railroad legislation was suppressed. In 1873 the Master of the Minnesota State Grange, being informed that certain Granges in his jurisdiction had appointed delegates to a State anti-railroad convention, ordered the offending Granges to recall their delegates. Congressman D. W. Aiken of South Carolina, long a member of the National Executive Committee, said in an address four year ago: "Frequently had the Grange to bear the odium of other men's sins. . . . For instance, there existed in Illinois and Wisconsin, and other sections of the Northwest, agricultural clubs whose province seemed to be to wage war against transportation companies. Anathemas were hurled upon the Grange for making this attack, whereas every Patron of Husbandry knew that the Grange as such was not a participant in the fight from beginning to end." It may seem surprising that such an error should have arisen, but it is not inexplicable. The newspapers first applied the name "Grangers" to to Western farmers in general, and consequently to those fighting railroads. From this it was an easy step to the assertion that the Grange was the fighting organization. There were some exceptions. The "Tribune" sent a special correspondent West, and afterward published a "Farmers' Extra," in which it is expressely recognized that the Grange is not fighting railroads, though some Grangers are. The "Times" published the same discovery with the comment that the general impression on this point was a mistaken one. But the "Nation," which talked loudest of all, and the press in general, made no such distinction. It is not strange that Mr. C. F. Adams and other writers on railroads have followed this leading, as it was of no consequence to them whether the Western agitators were known as "Grangers" or by any other name. The principal difficulty is with those who wrote from the farmers' standpoint. It can only be said that they wrote before the railroad legislation had been given a fair trial, and that they wanted to claim for the order the credit of what looked like a success. Their books, in general, are of a hortatory and prophetic rather than historical character. * * *

GRANGE AND RAILROAD LEGISLATION.

In spite of the assertions of Mr. C. F. Adams and others, it can be shown that the Grange was not responsible for the Illinois railroad legislation. When the Constitution of 1870 and the law of 1871 were passed, the Grange had scarcely a foothold in the state. The State Grange was organized in March, 1872. The real organ of agitation was the "State Farmers' Association," whose subordinate lodges were called "Farmers' Club." Its president, W. C. Flagg, testified before the Windom committee in 1873 that he was not a Granger, that his organization was an open and political one, while the Grange was secret and non-political, disavowing and preventing, as far as it could, any political action. By 1874 seven states had passed so-called "Granger" laws, either fixing maxima or providing for a commission to make out a schedule of rates.

Meanwhile cases were before the Supreme Court on the validity of all this legislation. The court recognized the gravity of the question and reserved its decision, affirming the constitutionality of the laws for more than a year after the test case (Munn vs. Illinois) was argued. The grist of the decision is in the following words: "When one devotes his property to a use in which the public has an interest, he, in effect, grants the public an interest in that use, and must submit to be controlled by the public for the common good to the extent of the interest he has thus created." The decisions in this, and the six other "Granger" cases, were pronounced by Chief-Justice Waite, Justices Field and Strong dissenting:

In the courts the farmers were victorious. But, unfortunately, the Supreme Court does not pass upon economic laws, and to these the movement had already succumbed. By the time the cases were decided, in 1876-77, scarcely one of the statutes in question remained in force. In the second year under the Potter law, no Wisconsin road paid a dividend, and only four paid interest on their bonds. Foreign capitalists refused to invest further in the state. On the recommendation of the Governor, the very men who had passed the law hurriedly repealed it. In the next year

Mr. Potter faded out of American politics, and his place in the Senate was filled by another. Most of the other states also beat a precipitate retreat, poorly covered by a faint demonstration against unreasonableness in general.

So the victors were beaten, and bad times made the defeat seem worse than it was. But they claim, and not without reason, to have done lasting good.

The founders of the Grange thought they were establishing an order whose aims were to be social and educational. But these were soon overshadowed by the co-operative, anti-middleman feature. This drew more into the order than all other considerations. Combined at one time almost threatening to transform our farming population into a race of traders, and this was likewise the chief cause of Grange decay. Fighting middlemen, unlike fighting railroads, was a legitimate kind of activity, as it had nothing to do with politics or theology—the two subjects tabooed by Granger law. Unfortunately, the story of Grange co-operation is recorded nowhere and thoroughly known to nobody. Those who know most preserve a discreet silence, mindful of questionable transactions and failures, now generally forgotten.

TOO MUCH OF A GOOD THING.

No sooner had Kelley established a few Granges in Minnesota in 1869 than they set up a clamor for leasing flouring mills and appointing agents in St. Paul and New York, in order to mill and ship their own grain. However farcical might be the position of the founders at Washington, they at least were conservative enough to disavow this action. But upon Minnesota's threat to secede they yielded, and an agent was appointed in St. Paul. His first commission chanced to be to buy a jackass for a Patron, whereupon one of the founders made comment: "This purchasing business commenced with buying asses; the prospects are that many will be sold." As soon as the National Grange fell into the hands of farmers, there was a movement to make it the head of a gigantic co-operative scheme. It was proposed to have three national purchasing agents, stationed at New York, Chicago and New Orleans, to buy for the Patrons of the whole country. But this was soon found impracticable, owing to the diversity of interests in the order. The same was true with regard to the purchase of patent-rights. With the view of absorbing into the order the profits of manufacturing farming implements, the National Grange had bought the right to manufacture a harvester, a mower and reaper, and various other machines. It had also tried to buy the copyright of Cushing's "Manual"—a book in great demand among the Granges. Meanwhile the Executive Committee was busy in another direction. Congressman Aiken of South Carolina, one of its members, says that they "visited the manufacturers who supplied the market with such implements as the farmers needed, from a scooter-plow to a parlor organ, proposing to concentrate the purchases of the order where the greatest discounts were obtained for cash. In no instance did they fail to secure a reduction of twenty-five to fifty per cent." Mr. Aiken notes the astonishment of one cutlery-maker of a single order for ten thousand pruning-knives of a particular pattern. Such enormous reductions from regular prices were obtained only under a pledge of secrecy. But as information had to be distributed by thousands of printed sheets, the Patrons could not keep the secret. The contracts leaked out, causing the withdrawal of many firms from their agreements.

What experiments the National Grange might have tried with the great sums in its treasury can only be conjectured, as its resources and influence over the subordinate lodges were crippled almost fatally in the Charleston meeting in 1875. It probably would have continued the crop reports, which, though costly, and often unreliable through the ignorance and carelessness of Granges and furnishing statistics, had proved valuable. Like the State Granges, which had full treasuries, it might have squandered its capital and come to grief on co-operative ventures. Such is the inference to be drawn from utterances like the following, from the Executive Committee: "To secure rights to manufacture leading implements . . . is pre-eminently a duty of the National Grange, and a measure of the greatest importance, directly, because the profits of manufacture will thus be controlled by the Order, as well as the profits of transfer or dealing; indirectly, by securing facilities that will favor the introduction of manufacturing establishments in districts at present far removed from them, and where their products are in demand." The plan of having the farmer's machinery manufactured at his door and under his supervision was much better as a statment of protectionist doctrine than as a guide to safe investment. The policy of the meeting of 1875 indicated that, before it was too late, the National Grange recognized that there was danger of going too fast, and that its province was rather to devise plans for the use of the order than to plunge into enterprises itself. It therefore sounded a note of caution, and first issuing a scheme for co-operative joint-stock stores based on something found in this country, proceeded to work out a more elaborate system on the model of the Rochdale Pioneers. Various English publications on co-operation were distributed among the order, and an envoy was sent to England to confer with English co-operators. The result was a new set of rules, closely following the Rochdale plan, and insisting on the feature of investing the profits of trade for the stockholders on the basis of purchases, as opposed to the simple joint-stock arrangement of the earlier scheme, which had been largely put in practice. After a prolonged stay, the commissioner to England made his report, bringing from English co-operators proposals for dealings on a great scale. The Grange was to subscribe one hundred and twenty-five thousand dollars toward the necessary shipping-depots, and all trade was to be carried on directly with England through a company to be known as the "Anglo-American Co-operative Company." The Englishmen followed the matter up by sending three men to the United States to confer with the Executive Committee. After looking over the ground, they proposed to erect their own warehouses at four seaboard cities, prepared to supply every article of clothing and every farm implement needed by Patrons at a discount of ten per cent, and to receive in exchange every variety of farm produce at the market price, provided that the Grange would concentrate its purchases upon them. But by this time the ardor of the Patrons had been cooled by reverses in local experiments, and the Executive Committee was unable to make the necessary guarantees. The National Grange's efforts now subsided into protests and warnings against the commission and joint-stock ventures so common in the order, and pleas for the Rochdale system. Many enterprises were undertaken upon this basis, proving, if not highly profitable, at least not disastrous. But in general, the warning came too late. The Patrons had been too impatient to grasp the anticipated gains, and had burned their fingers.

CO-OPERATIVE ENTERPRISES.

The step from co-operation in the National, to co-operation in the State and District Granges is one from theory tinged by practice, to practice pure and simple. The craze for co-operation was like that for gold in 1848. The first and simplest step was to appoint a profusion of buying and selling agents, usually on salaries from the State Granges. But a few losses by mismanagement and rascality were enough to deter the farmers from trusting their produce to selling agents. The system of agencies for buying only was not open to the same risks, but its utility differed in different states. For Iowa, where every farmer raised grain and wanted plows and reapers, an agent could buy to great advantage. The Patrons there gave figures to show that they saved fifty thousand dollars in one year on plows and cultivators alone. In the same year they bought fifteen hundred sewing machines, at a reduction of forty-five per cent from retail prices. Local dealers were driven out of business. In New York, on the other hand, where the farmers are dairymen, grain-growers, nurserymen, and hop-growers, a state buying-agency was found useless, and was abandoned, after some hard experience, for a system of district agencies. These have effected saving in some instances, in others proved unprofitable, partly owing to the outcroppings of mean human nature among those most clamorous for the benefits. The "State Women's Dress Agency," in New York city, lasted longer, but, strangely enough, the Patronesses preferred to buy their own dresses, and it finally expired. The states did not stop with agencies. They too began to buy patent-rights. There was an idea that all the principal machinery used by the order should be manufactured within it. Flouring-mills, elevators, tobacco and grain warehouses, were established. Some ventures were unsuccessful from the start, and at once clamored for subsidies. Others boasted of the greatest prosperity, one making a dividend of fifty per cent the first year. In 1874 two thirds of the elevators in Iowa were in Grange hands. The experiment of shipping provisions directly to Southern Grange centers was undertaken. In 1876 the Patrons were said to own five steamboats or packet lines, thirty-two grain elevators, and twenty-two warehouses. Some of these were local ventures, but the full treasuries of the State Granges furnished the capital for most of them. It is always easy to experiment with other men's money, and the State Grange officials found no difficulty in getting, with the Grange funds, into enterprises where disaster was inevitable. It came in every instance. The blow was so overwhelming in some states (Arkansas and Nebraska for example), that they dropped at once from the order. District Granges disbanded for fear of being held individually liable for State Grange debts, and the very name Granger became a reproach. In other states the Grange was greatly weakened, but survived. In Iowa a few hundred of the faithful have struggled on for years, the officers receiving no salaries, but devoting all receipts to the debt, left as a reminder of past glories.

DECADENCE OF THE GRANGE.

Much of the later history of the Grange has been anticipated in treating of railroad legislation and co-operation, but its decadence merits a little closer attention. Only those interested in agricultural pursuits were eligible for membership, but, in the unprecedented growth of the order under the labors of twelve hundred deputies, it was impossible to keep out men who were farmers only to the extent of a garden or back yard. In those days lawyers, doctors, merchants, discovered in themselves a marvelous interest in agricultural pursuits, and joined the Grange. As a Granger remarked, they were interested in agriculture as the hawk is interested in the sparrow. Two Granges were organized in New York city; one, the "Manhattan," on Broadway, with a membership of forty-five wholesale dealers, sewing machine manufacturers, etc., representing a capital of as many millions; the other, the "Knickerbocker," one of whose first official acts was to present the National Grange with a handsome copy of the Scriptures—a gift causing some embarrassment. A similar one was organized in Boston, which made great trouble before it could be expelled; and one was found in Jersey City, with a general of the army as its master, a stone-mason as secretary, and the owner of a grain elevator as chaplain. But discordant elements were not all from other professions. Thousands of farmers had been carried in by the enthusiasm of the movement, with no idea of the nature and aims of the order. Some expected to make a political party; others, to smash the railroads; almost all hoped to find in co-operation a panacea for poverty. There was great lack of discipline, but no discipline could have harmonized such a body. The first outbreak was in the direction of democracy. Lay members were eligible to but four of the seven degrees, and this was denounced as aristocratic, opposed to the spirit of democratic institutions. Along with this came the cry that the National Grange was growing too rich. In vain it made liberal donations of seeds and provisions to sufferers by grasshoppers and floods, and spent large sums in distributing crop reports among the order. The clamor continued till the faint-hearted in the Charleston session in 1875 carried a measure to distribute $55,000 to the subordinate Granges —about $2.50 to each! Prominent Grangers have maintained that the causes of Grange decay are to be found in this and the other measures of the same session curtailing the power of the National Grange. The true cause has been seen to lie deeper, in the failure of business enterprises. These measures had some influence, however. They were the beginning of endless tinkering with the constitution, and the cause of quarrels innumerable. Among other quarrels was one with the Grange of Canada, over the question of jurisdiction. Soon afterward came the first open break in the ranks. An Illinois Grange voted to disband, alleging pecuniary reasons and the autocratic rule of the National Grange. Many still had dreams that the order was to spread over the world, but the co-operative leaven had begun to work, and there was soon no mistaking the tendency to decay. At the annual meeting in 1876, four thousand Granges were reported delinquent. Salaries were at once reduced—the master's from $2,000 to $1,200, and the secretary's from $2,500 to $2,000. It was vainly attempted to stem the tide by issuing an official organ, the "Grange Record." In 1879 the master's salary was dropped entirely, and the secretary's reuced to $600. A bill for services from Herr Prenzel, who had been working for the order in Germany since 1875, was dismissed with little ceremony. The National Grange was not poor, having always kept about $50,000 to its credit invested in Government bonds, but it had given up the idea of converting the world.

But the low water mark had been reached. Cash receipts in 1880 increased two hundred per cent over those in 1879. More Granges had been organized than in any year since 1874. The growth was especially marked in New England. The State Grange of Connecticut was revived after a dormancy of six years, and Maine began to claim more Grangers in proportion to population than any other state. At the session of the National Grange for 1885, held in Boston, delegates were present from all the States and Territories but eight. It is not easy to explain this growth, as there seems to be no great principle underlying it. Some New England Patrons are agitating free trade, but that can not be called a Grange issue, as Pennsylvania Patrons want protection extended to farm products. The harmless practice of holding great fairs is gaining ground. At a recent one in Pennsylvania, lasting a week, the local paper says: "Over fifty thousand people were present on one day, and the sale of machinery direct to the farmers ran up into the hundreds of thousands of dollars. Never were manufacturers and consumers brought into more direct and friendly relations." This is, perhaps, the latest development of Grange anti-middleman ideas.

The most enthusiastic Grangers at present are the farmers' wives and daughters, who are attracted by the social opportunities. In fact the order seems to be going back to the educational and social basis of the founders, and its boasts are no longer cooperative ventures so much as Grange buildings and libraries, and the Grange schools that exist in several States. In these directions, and in what it has done to heal sectional differences between North and South, the Grange can boast its best achievements.

Address by Founder O. H. Kelly

Prepared for the Fortieth Anniversary of Fredonia Grange

No. 1 at Fredonia, N. Y. 1908

Worthy Masters and Patrons: I thank you for your compliments and assure you that it gives me great pleasure to be with you on this occasion. As Chautauqua county is historic ground in our Order, you will permit me to try to entertain you with a few reminiscences of the early days in our history.

I consider that all the work done in Washington was merely preliminary and that the actual work of establishing the Order commenced when I packed all the documents of the embryo National Grange in my gripsack and started out to tramp my way to Minnesota with the hope of organizing a sufficient number of subordinate Granges to defray the expenses of the trip

The day I started, I called upon Brother Saunders to bid him farewell, and I received his blessing in these impressive words: "You are a ——— fool to start on such a trip!" I had plenty of grit in these days—and the stock has not given out—such encouraging words rather stimulated than depressed me. After a few days of good, valuable experience on my way, I reached Fredonia. N. Y., and found good Brother A. S. Moss ready to receive me. On Thursday evening, April 16, 1868, I organized Fredonia Grange, and in so doing we laid the corner stone of the Order of Patrons of Husbandry and Brother Moss stands credited as the father of that grange. He was a "founder". I yet have the old ritual used on that occasion.

I reached Minnesota in just one month and have never had the least desire to repeat the trip; yet the information gained proved of value in after years—the "fool" had gained in wisdom. Twenty-five years after, Brother Dodge told me that I looked like a tramp when I came to organize Fredonia; my trip had not improved my appearance. In August of that year (1868) Sister Hall returned from Boston and commenced active work with me, as assistant in my office. In '69, I had increased the number of my acquaintances and had enlisted several good men in the work. Our constitution then warranted general deputies, with membership, in council and senate of the National Grange. The prospect of being recognized there proved an inducement to them to exert themselves in building up the order.

In July, 1870, I made the acquaintance of the Hon. Thomas B. Bryan of Chicago, who afterwards became an important factor in our work, and he was a "founder". He told me that the objects of the organization met with his approval, but that he did not see how he could assist me unless it might be with money as occasion might require. You have all seen a hungry dog grab a bone, haven't you? The sensations I enjoyed at that information were decidedly pleasant; the results I will mention later. As a coincidence, some 30 years after, it was good fortune, quite unexpected, to do him a far greater favor, which was appreciated.

In 1870 Miss Hall and I decided that the headquarters for our work should be in Washington. Our work was gradually increasing and we were satisfied that letters and documents, mailed from that city, received more respect and attention than those sent from our farm.

In January 1871 we moved. Mr. Bryan furnished me with the sum of $260, with which to move my family from Minnesota to Washington. It was a wild venture but the "fool" made the move. The results were evident in about six months. Granges were being organized and the general deputies were earning their reputations as faithful and earnest laborers in the good work. They were "founders" too. The year closed with 123 new granges against 38 the year previous. In February of 1871, I borrowed of Mr. Bryan $184 to enable me to settle with the printers and this placed the National Grange on the cash paying basis. Never since that date has the National Grange contracted a debt without having the money to meet the bill at sight. The "fool" was making his mark. The year 1873 opened with a bright sun and the work was proving a success. We closed that year with one thousand and seventy-four new granges.

Now came the time to call all the leaders together and to organize the National Grange permanently. Up to this time it had been something of a myth. Invitations were sent to all the general deputies and masters of State Granges which had been organized, for under the constitution then existing they were all entitled to full membership. I considered them as the real founders of the Order and presumed that they would be recognized as full members of the National Grange. In January 1873 all who could make it convenient to attend, met at my home in Georgetown. Seventeen of the twenty-seven I had counted on arrived. My associates in Washington, with the exception of Brother Ireland, were present; they were in session four days. The work done was the revision of the constitution and this was done in such a man-her that it put nearly all of those who had worked so faithfully into "cold storage". Only four, whom they elected to office, were recognized as belonging to the National Grange. This was a damper on Miss Hall and myself. Only the State Masters and their wives were entitled to votes. The Order was, in fact, under an entirely new Constitution. It is quite reasonable to suppose that those who had been thus unceremoniously "turned down" felt hurt. Most of them were my personal friends. I advised them to attend the next session at St. Louis, and see if some measure could be adopted for their reward. But nothing was accomplished for them.

I determined to write my history of the first five years of the existence of the Grange and to give every one full credit for what he or she had done. I had on file every letter which had been written to me and by publishing them would verify my statements over the writers' signatures. I decided to publish the most important of those letters and I did so a year later. The writers of the letters were all living when the book was published. It made quite a stir but, of all the letters published, the authenticity of one, only, was ever questioned; to convince the author of it, I had this letter photographed, actual size, and sent him two copies—that settled it. It contained these words: "I call it your Order for you not only conceived the idea but are making it go unaided and alone."

In my history, in order to give every one full credit, I published, not only their letters, but as far as possible, their photographs. I put their names on the Roll of Honor, and I supplemented that with a list of the names of one thousand nine hundred and twenty-five deputies, with the number of granges that each one hand organized.

Now, let me get back to old Fredonia. I am at home there. It is in that Grange that I am both a life and an honorary member; it is the only Grange in which Miss Hall or I have ever been entitled to a vote. We never have had the privilege of voting in the National Grange since the Georgetown session, in which it was decided that only Masters of State Granges and their wives should be entitled to votes in that body. I am told, however, that I am also a member of this Chautauqua Pomona. That being the case, I feel here that I am right in the family and, perhaps, some of the younger members here will be encouraged to persevere in good work, despite discouragement, if I note some of the results of the stubborn perseverance of one called a "fool"

When in 1867, I put the postage stamp on the first letter I ever sent in the interest of the Order, addressed to Anson Bartlett in Ohio, I made the first investment for the National Grange; six years and a half later we had deposited in the Farmers' Loan and Trust Co., in New York, $110,000 and there was not a cent of debt. If $50,000 of that amount had been invested in Washington property, which was offered to us at that time, it would today bring a return of fully $275,000—its present value; Instead, the money was given back to the States and there is no one living who can tell today of any practical good a single dollar of it ever did. From that "fool's" trip and the founding of Fredonia Grange over 24,000 subordinate Granges have received charters—surpassing any other organization ever established in this or any other country! At various times we had nearly 2,000 deputies in the work of organization and of that number only two were dishonest.

This recalls a huge joke that one member of the National

Grange played upon himself; he was one of those unfortunate people who could not see any honesty in any one—except himself. He knew that there had passed through my office over $350,000; for some reason he had a grudge against Miss Hall and myself and was confident that we could not have handled so large a sum without stealing some of it. He introduced a resolution asking that a committee be appointed to examine our books. The committee was appointed and he, of course, was the chairman. I think they were in session for two weeks and then gravely reported that the National Grange owed my office the sum of $8.40! I claim no credit for this. Miss Hall was the cashier of my office and all monies received passed through her hands. When the committee left, we immediately set an expert at work on the books, with the result we expected. His report showed that there was over $400 due the office and it was promptly paid.

The first year's work of organizing resulted in ten subordinate granges. Compare that record with that of two days in February 1874, when we received 165 applications each day and $15 with each application. making $2,475 a day. Now, if that was a part of the result of the labor of a "fool" you young folks with good, sound common sense may take courage and persevere.

History of the Grange Movement

Or the Farmers' War Against Monopolies

The above is the title of a large octavo volume of 534 pages, written in 1873 by E. W. Martin, which was "issued by subscription only and is not for sale in the book stores." It is long ago out of print and only scattering copies are now in existence. It is a most interesting work, the first 400 pages of which are given up to a detailed discussion of "Railroad Monopolies" and an account of the Farmers' Wrongs, and concludes with a History of the Order of Patrons of Husbandry.

The main facts of this History necessarily coincide with those given in the previous pages of this booklet and need not be here repeated, but there are some incidental touches of historic interest to which I will refer in the following paragraphs.

The historian says that the most remarkable growth of the Order was manifested in the State of Iowa "in which as many as 80 Granges per week were organized at one period of the present year," (1873). The number of subordinate granges in Iowa was then 1800 with a membership of nearly 100,000. It seems that it was the custom of the then Secretary of the National Grange, O. H. Kelley, to issue from his office in Washington, a weekly Bulletin showing the strength of the Order in each state. The total number of granges on Oct. 4, 1873 was 6914 "being an increase of 852 in a single month." From this particular Bulletin it appears that the number of subordinate granges in each state at that date was as follows: Alabama 94, Arkansas 61, California 75, Florida 10, Georgia 213, Illinois 652, Indiana 421, Iowa 1811, Kansas 577, Kentucky 9, Louisiana 24, Maryland 2, Massachusetts 5, Michigan 81, Minnesota 358, Mississippi 362, Missouri 872, Nebraska 327, New Hampshire 4, New Jersey 9, New York 11, North Carolina 96, Ohio 147, Oregon 35, Pennsylvania 26, South Carolina 161, Tennessee

158, Texas 23, Vermont 27, Virginia 3, West Virginia 16, Wisconsin 209, Colorado 2, Dakota 20, Washington 5, (Canada 8).

A comparison of these figures with those of the present day (1911) will show how great a change has been wrought in 38 years, in respect to the strength of the Order in the various states. Where the Order then flourished so conspicuously, now it is very weak, while in the states then weak, the Order is now strong. Speaking of the wonderful growth of the Grange at this time the New York Tribune had this to say:

It took its origin a few years ago in a Washington office. Its founders were not farmers, but government clerks. They understood, however, the temper and wants of the agricultural class, and they devised, with aid, perhaps, from the prairies, one of the most ingenious and effective organizations ever invented in so short a time. From Washington the Grange spread all over the great grain region and back again to the far East and southward into the country of cotton and tobacco. Everywhere it found enthusiastic adherents. Everywhere it found farmers who needed its help, farmers' wives and daughters, who picked up new life and a fresh spirit under its social and intellectual influence, and gave it in return the attraction of a refined and cheerful membership. Business and pleasure surely were never so profitably combined before. It was the old principle of the husking frolic and the quilting bee, applied to loftier objects and practiced with a sterner eye to the main chance. The women and the young people, who met at evenings to go through the little ceremonies of the grangers' ritual, and pass an hour or so in decorous amusements and conversation, and song, and reading, may have fancied that they were only breaking the monotony of toil by a bit of harmless entertainment; but the grange knew better. They were learning, and teaching others, to be better farmers, to be thrifty, to buy cheaper, to sell better, to rid themselves of creditors, to keep out of debt, and finally to check the enormous power of the railroads which have so long been driving the farmers to the wall. In fact, the grange succeeded so well because it had the art to take the average men and women of the West and make them work without knowing it, and accomplish what they hardly dreamed of. That it did succeed is a sufficient evidence that it was founded upon a genuine and general popular need, and directed toward a really important object. Even if it should be worsted at last in the struggle against monopoly, it will still have done ample good to justify its existence. J. W. D.

OFFICERS OF THE NATIONAL GRANGE.

From the Foundation of the Order to the Year 1911.

Worthy Master.

William Saunders, Washington, D. C., Dec., 1867, to Jan., 1873.
 uary, 1873.

D. W. Adams, Iowa, January, 1873, to November, 1875.
J. T. Jones, Arkansas, November, 1875, to November, 1877.
S. E. Adams, Minnesota, November, 1877, to November, 1879.
F. J. Woodman, Michigan, November, 1879, to November, 1885.
Put. Darden, Mississippi, Nov., 1885, to death, July 17, 1888.
James Draper, Massachusetts, July 17, 1888, to Nov., 1888.
J. H. Brigham, Ohio, November, 1888, to November, 1897.

Aaron Jones, November, 1897, to November, 1905.
N. J. Bachelder, New Hampshire, November, 1905, to present.

Worthy Overseer.

Anson Bartlett, Ohio, December 3, 1867, to January, 1873.
Thomas Taylor, South Carolina, January, 1873, to Nov., 1875.
J. J. Woodman, November, 1875, to November, 1879.
Put. Darden, Mississippi, November, 1879, to November, 1885.
James Draper, Massachusetts, November, 1885, to Nov. 1889.
Hiram Hawkins, Alabama, November, 1889, to November, 1891.
E. W. Davis, California, November, 1891, to November, 1895.
Aaron Jones, Indiana, November, 1895, to November, 1897.
O. H. Hale, New York, November, 1897, to November, 1899.
O. Gardner, Maine, November, 1899, to November, 1903.
T. C. Atkeson, West Virginia, November, 1903, to present.

Worthy Lecturer.

J. R. Thompson, Washington, D. C., Dec., 1867, to Jan. 1872.
D. W. Adams, Iowa, Jan., 1872, to Jan., 1873.
T. A. Thompson, Minnesota, January, 1873, to November, 1875.
A. B. Smedley, Iowa, November, 1875, to November, 1877.
M. Whitehead, New Jersey, November, 1877, to Nov., 1879.
H. Eshbaugh, Missouri, November, 1879, to November, 1885.
M. Whitehead, New Jersey, November, 1885, to November, 1893.
A. Messer, Vermont, November, 1893, to November, 1899.
N. J. Bachelder, New Hampshire, Nov., 1899, to Nov., 1905.
George W. F.Gaunt, New Jersey, Nov., 1905, to Nov., 1909.
Oliver Wilson, Illinois, November, 1909, to present.

Worthy Steward.

William Muir, Missouri, Dec. 4, 1867, to Jan., 1873.
A. J. Vaughn, Mississippi, Jan., 1873, to Nov., 1881.
William Sims, Kansas, Nov., 1881, to Nov., 1885.
J. E. Hall, West Virginia, Nov., 1885, to Nov., 1887.
X. X. Charters, Virginia, Nov., 1887, to Nov., 1889.
E. W. Davis, California, Nov., 1889, to Nov., 1891.
A. E. Page, Missouri, Nov., 1891, to Nov., 1893.
M. B. Hunt, Maine, Nov., 1893, to Nov., 1895.
J. T. Cox, New Jersey, Nov., 1899, to Nov., 1903.
W. C. Jewett, Massachusetts, Nov., 1895, to Nov., 1899.
J. A. Newcomb, Colorado, Nov., 1903, to Nov., 1909.
C. D. Richardson, Massachusetts, Nov., 1909, to present.

Worthy Assistant Steward.

A. S. Moss, New York, Dec. 4, 1867, to Jan., 1873.
G. W. Thompson, New Jersey, Jan., 1873, to Nov., 1875.
M. Whitehead, New Jersey, Nov., 1875, to Nov., 1877.
William Sims, Kansas, Nov., 1877, to Nov., 1881.
J. J. Rosa, Delaware, Nov., 1881, to Nov., 1885.
W. H. Stinson, New Hampshire, Nov., 1885, to Nov., 1887.
J. H. Hale, Connecticut, Nov., 1887, to Nov., 1889.
O. E. Hall, Nebraska, Nov., 1889, to Nov., 1893.
A. M. Belcher, Rhode Island, Nov., 1893, to Nov., 1905.
J. A. Newcomb, Colorado, Nov., 1895, to Nov., 1901.
C. O. Raine, Missouri, Nov., 1901, to Nov., 1903.
G. W. F. Gaunt, New Jersey, Nov., 1903, to Nov., 1905.
C. D. Richardson, Massachusetts, Nov., 1905, to Nov., 1909.
L. H. Healey, Connecticut, Nov., 1909, to present.

Worthy Chaplain.

A. B. Grosh, Washington, Dec., 1867, to Nov., 1875.
S. H. Ellis, Ohio, Nov., 1875, to Nov., 1877.
A. P. Forsythe, Illinois, Nov., 1877, to Nov., 1879.
S. H. Ellis, Ohio, Nov., 1879, to Nov., 1881.
H. O. Devries, Maryland, Nov., 1881, to Nov., 1885.
A. J. Rose, Texas, Nov., 1885, to Nov., 1891.
Charles McDaniel, New Hampshire, Nov., 1891, to Nov., 1893.
S. L. Wilson, Mississippi, Nov., 1893, to Nov., 1895.
O. H. Hale, New York, Nov., 1895, to Nov., 1897.
S. O. Bowen, Connecticut, Nov., 1897, to Nov., 1901.
W. K. Thompson, South Carolina, Nov., 1901, to Nov., 1907.
O. S. Wood, Connecticut, Nov., 1907, to Nov., 1909.
C. F. Smith, Vermont, Nov., 1909, to present.

Worthy Treasurer.

W. M. Ireland, Washington, D. C., Dec., 1867, to Jan., 1872.
J. R. Thompson, Washington, D. C., Jan. 1872, to Jan., 1873.
F. M. McDowell, New York, Jan., 1873, to Nov., 1893.
Mrs. L. S. McDowell, New York, Nov., 1893, to present.

Worthy Secretary.

O. H. Kelley, Minnesota, Dec., 1867, to Nov., 1878.
W. M. Ireland, Washington, D. C., Nov., 1878, to Nov., 1885.
John Trimble, Washington, D. C., Nov., 1885, to death, December, 30, 1902.
C. M. Freeman, Ohio, Jan., 3, 1903, to present.

Worthy Gate Keeper.

E. P. Tarvis, reidence and time of service unknown.
O. Dunwiddie, Indiana, Jan., 1873, to Nov., 1881.
J. V. Scott, Arkansas, Nov., 1881, to Nov., 1883.
James Draper, Massachusetts, Nov., 1883, to Nov., 1885.
H. Thompson, Delaware, Nov., 1885, to Nov., 1887.
A. N. Brown, Delaware, Nov., 1887, to Nov., 1889.
A. E. Page, Missouri, Nov., 1889, to Nov., 1891.
W. H. Nelson, Tennessee, Nov., 1891, to Nov., 1893.
W. E. Harbaugh, Missouri, Nov., 1893, to Nov., 1897.
A. B. Judson, Iowa, Nov., 1897, to Nov., 1899.
H. E. Huxley, Wisconsin, Nov., 1899, to Nov., 1901.
G. W. Baird, Minnesota, Nov., 1901, to Nov., 1903.
B. C. Patterson, Connecticut, Nov., 1903, to Nov., 1905.
A. C. Powers, Wisconsin, Nov., 1905, to Nov., 1909.
D. C. Mullen, Idaho, Nov., 1909, to present.

Worthy Ceres.

Mrs. D. W. Adams, Iowa, Jan., 1873, to Nov., 1875.
Mrs. J. T. Jones, Arkansas, Nov., 1875, to Nov., 1877.
Mrs. S. E. Adams, Minnesota, Nov., 1877, to Nov., 1879.
Mrs. J. J. Woodman, Michigan, Nov., 1879, to Nov., 1885.
Mrs. K. A. Darden, Mississippi, Nov., 1885, to Nov., 1889.
Mrs. J. H. Brigham, Ohio, Nov., 1889, to Nov., 1893.
Mrs. M. S. Rhone, Pennsylvania, Nov., 1893, to Nov., 1895.
Mrs. L. G. Smith, Ohio, Nov., 1895, to Nov., 1897.
Mrs. L. M. Messick, Delaware, Nov., 1897, to Nov., 1899.
Mrs. C. M. Atkeson, West Virgina, Nov., 1899, to Nov., 1901.
Mrs. M. M. Wilson, Illinois, Nov., 1901, to Nov., 1905.
Mrs. C. R. F. Ladd, Massachusetts, Nov., 1905, to Nov., 1907.
Mrs. Elizabeth H. Patterson, Maryland, Nov., 1907 to present.

Worthy Pomona.

Mrs. O. H. Kelley, Washington, D. C., Jan., 1873, to Feb., 1874.
Mrs. Thomas Taylor, South Carolina, Feb., 1874, to Nov., 1875.
Mrs. H. Goddard, Connecticut, Nov., 1875, to Nov., 1877.
Mrs. J. J. Woodman, Michigan, Nov., 1877, to Nov., 1879.
Mrs. M. L. Darden, Mississippi, Nov., 1879, to Nov., 1884.
Mrs. S. J. Blanton, Virginia, Nov., 1884, to Nov., 1885.
Mrs. S. H. Neal, Kentucky, Nov., 1885, to Nov., 1889.
Mrs. M. J. Thompson, Nov., 1889, to Nov., 1891.
Mrs. C. E. Bowen, Connecticut, Nov., 1891, to Nov., 1893.
Mrs. M. M. Rarden, Kansas, Nov., 1893, to Nov., 1895.
Mrs. S. G. Baird, Minnesota, Nov., 1895, to Nov., 1899.
Mrs. M. M. Wilson, Illinois, Nov., 1899, to Nov., 1901.
Mrs. C. M. Atkeson, West Virginia, Nov., 1899, to Nov., 1901.
Mrs. E. M. Derby, Delaware, Nov., 1903, to Nov., 1907.
Mrs. Sarah G. Baird, Minnesota, Nov., 1907, to present.

Worthy Flora.

Mrs. J. C. Abbott, Iowa, Jan., 1873, to Feb., 1874.
Mrs. J. T. Moore, Maryland, Feb., 1874, to Nov., 1875.
Mrs. S. E. Adams, Minnesota, Nov., 1875, to Nov., 1877.
Mrs. J. T. Moore, Maryland, Nov. 1877, to Nov., 1879.
Mrs. E. M. Nicholson, New Jersey, Nov., 1879, to Nov., 1885.
Mrs. J. C. Draper, Massachusetts, Nov., 1885, to Nov., 1887.
Mrs. M. E. Luce, Michigan, Nov., 1887, to Nov., 1889.
Mrs. Joseph Bailey, Mississippi, Nov., 1889, to Nov., 1891.
Mrs. E. P. Wilson, Mississippi, Nov., 1891, to Nov., 1893.
Mrs. A. L. Bull, Minnesota, Nov., 1893, to Nov., 1895.
Mrs. E. L. A. Wiggin, Maine, Nov., 1895, to Nov., 1899.
Mrs. Ida V. High, Washington, Nov., 1899, to Nov., 1901.
Mrs. S. B. Wolcott, Kentucky, Nov., 1901, to Nov., 1903.
Mrs. P. F. Raine, Missouri, Nov., 1903, to Nov., 1905.
Mrs. Amanda M. Horton, Michigan, Nov., 1905, to Nov., 1907.
Mrs. Ida Judson, Iowa, Nov., 1907, to present.

Worthy Lady Assistant Steward.

Miss C. A. Hall, Minnesota, Jan., 1873, to Nov., 1879.
Mrs. H. A. Sims, Kansas, Nov., 1879, to Nov., 1885.
Mrs. E. M. Lipscomb, South Carolina, Nov., 1885, to Nov., 1887.
Mrs. H. A. Sims, Kansas, Nov., 1887, to Nov., 1889.
Mrs. L. C. Douglas, Massachusetts, Nov., 1889, to Nov., 1893.
Mrs. G. B. Horton, Michigan, Nov., 1893, to Nov., 1895.
Mrs. S. G. Knott, West Virginia, Nov., 1895, to Nov., 1897.
Mrs. G. B. Horton, Michigan, Nov., 1897, to Nov., 1901.
Mrs. W. F. Hill, Pennsylvania, Nov., 1901, to Nov., 1903.
Mrs. H. C. Raap, California, Nov., 1903, to Nov., 1905.
Mrs Joanna Walker, Delaware, Nov., 1905, to Nov., 1907.
Mrs. Mary H. Smith, Vermont, Nov., 1907, to present.